Workshop on Applications of Tree Automata Techniques in Natural Language Processing 2012

(ATANLP 2012)

Held at the 13th Conference of the European Chapter of the Association for Computational Linguistics (EACL 2012)

Avignon, France
23 – 27 April 2012

ISBN: 978-1-62276-491-4

Printed from e-media with permission by:

Curran Associates, Inc.
57 Morehouse Lane
Red Hook, NY 12571

CURRAN ASSOCIATES INC.
proceedings
.com

Some format issues inherent in the e-media version may also appear in this print version.

Printed by Curran Associates, Inc. (2012)

Association for Computational Linguistics
209 N. Eighth Street
Stroudsburg, Pennsylvania 18360

Phone: 1-570-476-8006
Fax: 1-570-476-0860

acl@aclweb.org

Additional copies of this publication are available from:

Curran Associates, Inc.
57 Morehouse Lane
Red Hook, NY 12571 USA
Phone: 845-758-0400
Fax: 845-758-2634
Email: curran@proceedings.com
Web: www.proceedings.com

Preface

We are very pleased to present the proceedings of the EACL 2012 Workshop on Applications of Tree Automata Techniques in Natural Language Processing (ATANLP 2012), held on April 24 in Avignon, France. The first ATANLP workshop was held two years ago in Uppsala, Sweden, in connection with the 48th Annual Meeting of the Association for Computational Linguistics. This year, ATANLP is conducted as a workshop of the 13th Conference of the European Chapter of the Association for Computational Linguistics.

The theory of tree automata has always had a close connection with natural language processing. In the 1960s, computational linguistics was the major driving force for the development of a theory of tree automata. Nevertheless, the number of successful applications of this theory to natural language processing remained small during the 20th century. During the last decade, the situation has started to change, and the change accelerates. Applications of tree automata in natural language processing can be found in work on topics as diverse as grammar formalisms, computational semantics, language generation, and machine translation. Researchers in natural language processing have recognized the usefulness of tree automata theory for solving the problems they are interested in, and theorists are inspired by the resulting theoretical questions.

The goals of this workshop are to provide a dedicated venue for the presentation of work that relates the tree automata techniques to natural language processing, and to create a forum where researchers from the two areas can meet and exchange ideas. Specifically, the workshop aims at raising the awareness for theoretical results useful for applications in natural language processing, and at identifying open theoretical problems raised by such applications.

We are very happy that Andreas Maletti (University of Stuttgart, Germany), an expert in the area of weighted tree automata and their application to natural language processing problems, agreed to present the invited lecture of the workshop. In addition the the invited talk and the presentations of four regular papers, the workshop features two tutorials given by Alexander Koller and Heiko Vogler. The workshop is concluded by an open problem session that, as we hope and believe, will provide an inspiring outlook on possible venues for future research.

We thank the members of the program committee for their support, and in particular for being careful reviewers of the papers submitted. Furthermore, we would like to thank the program committee chairs, Mirella Lapata and Lluís Màrquez, as well as the workshop chairs, Kristiina Jokinen and Alessandro Moschitti, for their friendly and professional assistance.

We hope that all participants of the workshop experience an inspiring event characterized by curiosity and an open-minded atmosphere, and that all readers of these proceedings will gain new insights that make a difference.

Frank Drewes
Marco Kuhlmann
March 2012

Organizers:

Frank Drewes, Umeå University (Sweden)
Marco Kuhlmann, Uppsala University (Sweden)

Program Committee:

Parosh Aziz Abdulla, Uppsala University (Sweden)
Leonor Becerra-Bonache, Université Jean Monnet (France)
Johanna Björklund, Umeaa University (Sweden)
David Chiang, ISI/University of Southern California (USA)
Loek Cleophas, Eindhoven University of Technology (The Netherlands)
François Denis, LIF Marseille (France)
Laura Kallmeyer, University of Düsseldorf (Germany)
Kevin Knight, ISI/University of Southern California (USA)
Alexander Koller, University of Potsdam (Germany)
Sebastian Maneth, NICTA and University of New South Wales (Australia)
Brink van der Merwe, Stellenbosch University (South Africa)
Mark-Jan Nederhof, University of St Andrews (UK)
Joachim Niehren, INRIA Lille (France)
Kai Salomaa, Queen's University (Canada)
Marc Tommasi, INRIA Lille (France)
Heiko Vogler, Technische Universität Dresden (Germany)

Invited Speaker:

Andreas Maletti, University of Stuttgart (Germany)

Presenters of Tutorials:

Alexander Koller, University of Potsdam (Germany)
Heiko Vogler, TU Dresden (Germany)

Table of Contents

Conference Program

Tuesday, April 24, 2012

8:45-9:00	Opening
9:00–10:00	Invited Talk: Multi Bottom-up Tree Transducers by Andreas Maletti
10:00–10:30	Coffee Break
	Paper Presentations
10:30–11:00	*Preservation of Recognizability for Weighted Linear Extended Top-Down Tree Transducers* Nina Seemann, Daniel Quernheim, Fabienne Braune and Andreas Maletti
11:00–11:30	*Deciding the Twins Property for Weighted Tree Automata over Extremal Semifields* Matthias Büchse and Anja Fischer
11:30–12:00	*TTT: A Tree Transduction Language for Syntactic and Semantic Processing* Adam Purtee and Lenhart Schubert
12:00–12:30	*Second Position Clitics and Monadic Second-Order Transduction* Neil Ashton
	Lunch
14:30–15:30	Tutorial: Weighted Recognizable Tree Languages – A Survey by Heiko Vogler
15:30–16:00	Coffee Break
16:00–17:00	Tutorial: Interpreted Regular Tree Grammars by Alexander Koller
17:00–17:30	Open Problems
17:30	Closing

Preservation of Recognizability for Weighted Linear Extended Top-Down Tree Transducers*

Nina Seemann and **Daniel Quernheim** and **Fabienne Braune** and **Andreas Maletti**
University of Stuttgart, Institute for Natural Language Processing
{seemanna,daniel,braunefe,maletti}@ims.uni-stuttgart.de

Abstract

An open question in [FÜLÖP, MALETTI, VOGLER: Weighted extended tree transducers. *Fundamenta Informaticae* 111(2), 2011] asks whether weighted linear extended tree transducers preserve recognizability in countably complete commutative semirings. In this contribution, the question is answered positively, which is achieved with a construction that utilizes *inside weights*. Due to the completeness of the semiring, the inside weights always exist, but the construction is only effective if they can be effectively determined. It is demonstrated how to achieve this in a number of important cases.

1 Introduction

Syntax-based statistical machine translation (Knight, 2007) created renewed interest in tree automata and tree transducer theory (Fülöp and Vogler, 2009). In particular, it sparked research on extended top-down tree transducers (Graehl et al., 2009), which are top-down tree transducers (Rounds, 1970; Thatcher, 1970) in which the left-hand sides can contain several (or no) input symbols. A recent contribution by Fülöp et al. (2011) investigates the theoretical properties of weighted extended tree transducers over countably complete and commutative semirings (Hebisch and Weinert, 1998; Golan, 1999). Such semirings permit sums of countably many summands, which still obey the usual associativity, commutativity, and distributivity laws. We will use the same class of semirings.

Input → [Parser] → [TM] → [LM] → Output

Figure 1: Syntax-based machine translation pipeline.

Extended top-down tree transducers are used as translation models (TM) in syntax-based machine translation. In the standard pipeline (see Figure 1; LM is short for language model) the translation model is applied to the parses of the input sentence, which can be represented as a recognizable weighted forest (Fülöp and Vogler, 2009). In practice, only the best or the n-best parses are used, but in principle, we can use the recognizable weighted forest of all parses. In either case, the translation model transforms the input trees into a weighted forest of translated output trees. A class of transducers preserves recognizability if for every transducer of the class and each recognizable weighted forest, this weighted forest of translated output trees is again recognizable. Fülöp et al. (2011) investigates which extended top-down tree transducers preserve recognizability under forward (i.e., the setting previously described) and backward application (i.e., the setting, in which we start with the output trees and apply the inverse of the translation model), but the question remained open for forward application of weighted linear extended top-down tree transducers [see Table 1 for an overview of the existing results for forward application due to Engelfriet (1975) in the unweighted case and Fülöp et al. (2010) and Fülöp et al. (2011) for the weighted case]. In conclusion, Fülöp et al. (2011) ask: "Are there a commutative semiring S that is countably complete wrt. $\sum$, a linear wxtt $\mathcal{M}$ [weighted extended top-down tree transducer with regular look-ahead; see Section 4], and a recognizable

* All authors were financially supported by the EMMY NOETHER project MA / 4959 / 1-1 of the German Research Foundation (DFG).

model		preserves regularity
unweighted	ln-XTOP	✓
	l-XTOP	✓
	l-XTOP^{R}	✓
	XTOP	✗
weighted	ln-XTOP	✓
	l-XTOP	[✓]
	l-XTOP^{R}	[✓]
	XTOP	✗

Table 1: Overview of the known results due to Engelfriet (1975) and Fülöp et al. (2011) and our results in boxes.

weighted tree language φ such that $\mathcal{M}(\varphi)$ [forward application] is not recognizable? Or even harder, are there S and $\mathcal{M}$ with the same properties such that $\mathcal{M}(\widetilde{1})$ [$\widetilde{1}$ is the weighted forest in which each tree has weight 1] is not recognizable?"

In this contribution, we thus investigate preservation of recognizability (under forward application) for linear extended top-down tree transducers with regular look-ahead (Engelfriet, 1977), which are equivalent to linear weighted extended tree transducers by Fülöp et al. (2011). We show that they always preserve recognizability, thus confirming the implicit hypothesis of Fülöp et al. (2011). The essential tool for our construction is the inside weight (Lari and Young, 1990; Graehl et al., 2008) of the states of the weighted tree grammar (Alexandrakis and Bozapalidis, 1987) representing the parses. The inside weight of a state q is the sum of all weights of trees accepted in this state. In our main construction (see Section 5) we first compose the input weighted tree grammar with the transducer (input restriction). This is particularly simple since we just abuse the look-ahead of the initial rules. In a second step, we normalize the obtained transducer, which yields the standard product construction typically used for input restriction. Finally, we project to the output by basically eliminating the left-hand sides. In this step, the inside weights of states belonging to deleted subtrees are multiplied to the production weight. Due to the completeness of the semiring, the inside weights always exist, but the infinite sums have to be computed effectively for the final step of the construction to be effective. This problem is addressed in Section 6, where we show several methods to effectively compute or approximate the inside weights for all states of a weighted tree grammar.

2 Notation

Our weights will be taken from a commutative semiring $(A, +, \cdot, 0, 1)$, which is an algebraic structure of two commutative monoids $(A, +, 0)$ and $(A, \cdot, 1)$ such that $\cdot$ distributes over $+$ and $0 \cdot a = 0$ for all $a \in A$. An infinitary sum operation $\sum$ is a family $(\sum_I)_I$ where I is a countable index set and $\sum_I : A^I \to A$. Given $f : I \to A$, we write $\sum_{i \in I} f(i)$ instead of $\sum_I f$. The semiring together with the infinitary sum operation $\sum$ is *countably complete* (Eilenberg, 1974; Hebisch and Weinert, 1998; Golan, 1999; Karner, 2004) if for all countable sets I and $a_i \in A$ with $i \in I$

- $\sum_{i \in I} a_i = a_m + a_n$ if $I = \{m, n\}$,
- $\sum_{i \in I} a_i = \sum_{j \in J}(\sum_{i \in I_j} a_i)$ if $I = \bigcup_{j \in J} I_j$ for countable sets J and I_j with $j \in J$ such that $I_j \cap I_{j'} = \emptyset$ for all different $j, j' \in J$, and
- $a \cdot (\sum_{i \in I} a_i) = \sum_{i \in I}(a \cdot a_i)$ for all $a \in A$.

For such a semiring, we let $a^* = \sum_{i \in \mathbb{N}} a^i$ for every $a \in A$. In the following, we assume that $(A, +, \cdot, 0, 1)$ is a commutative semiring that is countably complete with respect to $\sum$.

Our trees have node labels taken from an alphabet Σ and leaves might also be labeled by elements of a set V. Given a set T, we write $\Sigma(T)$ for the set

$$\{\sigma(t_1, \ldots, t_k) \mid k \in \mathbb{N}, \sigma \in \Sigma, t_1, \ldots, t_k \in T\} .$$

The set $T_\Sigma(V)$ of Σ-trees with V-leaves is defined as the smallest set T such that $V \cup \Sigma(T) \subseteq T$. We write T_Σ for $T_\Sigma(\emptyset)$. For each tree $t \in T_\Sigma(V)$ we identify nodes by positions. The root of t has position ε and the position iw with $i \in \mathbb{N}$ and $w \in \mathbb{N}^*$ addresses the position w in the i-th direct subtree at the root. The set of all positions in t is $\mathrm{pos}(t)$. We write $t(w)$ for the label (taken from $\Sigma \cup V$) of t at position $w \in \mathrm{pos}(t)$. Similarly, we use $t|_w$ to address the subtree of t that is rooted in position w, and $t[u]_w$ to represent the tree that is obtained from replacing the subtree $t|_w$ at w by $u \in T_\Sigma(V)$. For a given set $L \subseteq \Sigma \cup V$ of labels, we let

$$\mathrm{pos}_L(t) = \{w \in \mathrm{pos}(t) \mid t(w) \in L\}$$

be the set of all positions whose label belongs to L. We also write $\text{pos}_l(t)$ instead of $\text{pos}_{\{l\}}(t)$.

We often use the set $X = \{x_1, x_2, \dots\}$ of variables and its finite subsets $X_k = \{x_1, \dots, x_k\}$ for every $k \in \mathbb{N}$ to label leaves. Let V be a set potentially containing some variables of X. The tree $t \in T_\Sigma(V)$ is *linear* if $|\text{pos}_x(t)| \leq 1$ for every $x \in X$. Moreover, $\text{var}(t) = \{x \in X \mid \text{pos}_x(t) \neq \emptyset\}$ collects all variables that occur in t. Given a finite set Q and $T \subseteq T_\Sigma(V)$, we let

$$Q[T] = \{q(t) \mid q \in Q, t \in T\} \ .$$

We will treat elements of $Q[T]$ (in which elements of Q are always used as unary symbols) as special trees of $T_{\Sigma \cup Q}(V)$. A substitution θ is a mapping $\theta \colon X \to T_\Sigma(V)$. When applied to $t \in T_\Sigma(V)$, it returns the tree $t\theta$, which is obtained from t by replacing all occurrences of $x \in X$ (in parallel) by $\theta(x)$. This can be defined recursively by $x\theta = \theta(x)$ for all $x \in X$, $v\theta = v$ for all $v \in V \setminus X$, and $\sigma(t_1, \dots, t_k)\theta = \sigma(t_1\theta, \dots, t_k\theta)$ for all $\sigma \in \Sigma$ and $t_1, \dots, t_k \in T_\Sigma(V)$.

3 Weighted Tree Grammars

In this section, we will recall weighted tree grammars (Alexandrakis and Bozapalidis, 1987) [see (Fülöp and Vogler, 2009) for a modern treatment and a complete historical account]. In general, weighted tree grammars (WTGs) offer an efficient representation of weighted forests, which are sets of trees such that each individual tree is equipped with a weight. The representation is even more efficient than packed forests (Mi et al., 2008) and moreover can represent an infinite number of weighted trees. To avoid confusion between the nonterminals of a parser, which produces the forests considered here, and our WTGs, we will refer to the nonterminals of our WTG as *states*.

Definition 1. A *weighted tree grammar* (WTG) is a system (Q, Σ, q_0, P) where

- Q is a finite set of states (nonterminals),
- Σ is the alphabet of symbols,
- $q_0 \in Q$ is the starting state, and
- P is a finite set of productions $q \xrightarrow{a} t$, where $q \in Q$, $a \in A$, and $t \in T_\Sigma(Q)$. □

Example 2. We illustrate our notation on the WTG $G_{\text{ex}} = (Q, \Sigma, q_s, P)$ where

- $Q = \{q_s, q_{np}, q_{prp}, q_n, q_{adj}\}$,
- Σ contains "S", "NP", "VP", "PP", "DT", "NN", "N", "VBD", "PRP", "ADJ", "man", "hill", "telescope", "laughs", "the", "on", "with", "old", and "young", and
- P contains the productions

$$q_s \xrightarrow{1.0} \text{S}(q_{np}, \text{VP}(\text{VBD}(\text{laughs}))) \quad (\rho_1)$$
$$q_{np} \xrightarrow{0.4} \text{NP}(q_{np}, \text{PP}(q_{prp}, q_{np}))$$
$$q_{np} \xrightarrow{0.6} \text{NP}(\text{DT}(\text{the}), q_n) \quad (\rho_2)$$
$$q_{prp} \xrightarrow{0.5} \text{PRP}(\text{on})$$
$$q_{prp} \xrightarrow{0.5} \text{PRP}(\text{with})$$
$$q_n \xrightarrow{0.3} \text{N}(q_{adj}, q_n)$$
$$q_n \xrightarrow{0.3} \text{NN}(\text{man}) \quad (\rho_3)$$
$$q_n \xrightarrow{0.2} \text{NN}(\text{hill})$$
$$q_n \xrightarrow{0.2} \text{NN}(\text{telescope})$$
$$q_{adj} \xrightarrow{0.5} \text{ADJ}(\text{old})$$
$$q_{adj} \xrightarrow{0.5} \text{ADJ}(\text{young})$$

It produces a weighted forest representing sentences about young and old men with telescopes on hills. □

In the following, let $G = (Q, \Sigma, q_0, P)$ be a WTG. For every production $\rho = q \xrightarrow{a} t$ in P, we let $\text{wt}_G(\rho) = a$. The semantics of G is defined with the help of derivations. Let $\xi \in T_\Sigma(Q)$ be a sentential form, and let $w \in \text{pos}_Q(\xi)$ be such that w is the lexicographically smallest Q-labeled position in ξ. Then $\xi \Rightarrow_G^\rho \xi[t]_w$ if $\xi(w) = q$. For a sequence $\rho_1, \dots, \rho_n \in P$ of productions, we let $\text{wt}_G(\rho_1 \cdots \rho_n) = \prod_{i=1}^n \text{wt}_G(\rho_i)$. For every $q \in Q$ and $t \in T_\Sigma(Q)$, we let

$$\text{wt}_G(q, t) = \sum_{\substack{\rho_1, \dots, \rho_n \in P \\ q \Rightarrow_G^{\rho_1} \cdots \Rightarrow_G^{\rho_n} t}} \text{wt}_G(\rho_1 \cdots \rho_n) \ .$$

The WTG G computes the weighted forest $L_G \colon T_\Sigma \to A$ such that $L_G(t) = \text{wt}_G(q_0, t)$ for every $t \in T_\Sigma$. Two WTGs are equivalent if they compute the same weighted forest. Since productions of weight 0 are useless, we often omit them.

Example 3. For the WTG G_{ex} of Example 2 we display a derivation with weight 0.18 for the sentence "the man laughs" in Figure 2. □

The notion of inside weights (Lari and Young, 1990) is well-established, and Maletti and Satta

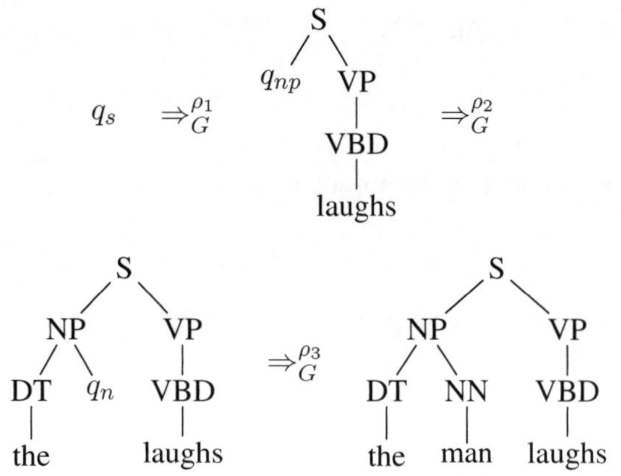

Figure 2: Derivation with weight $1.0 \cdot 0.6 \cdot 0.3$.

(2009) consider them for WTGs. Let us recall the definition.

Definition 4. The *inside weight* of state $q \in Q$ is

$$\mathrm{in}_G(q) = \sum_{t \in T_\Sigma} \mathrm{wt}_G(q, t) \ . \qquad \square$$

In Section 6 we demonstrate how to compute inside weights. Finally, let us introduce WTGs in normal form. The WTG G is in *normal form* if $t \in \Sigma(Q)$ for all its productions $q \xrightarrow{a} t$ in P. The following theorem was proven by Alexandrakis and Bozapalidis (1987) as Proposition 1.2.

Theorem 5. For every WTG there exists an equivalent WTG in normal form. □

Example 6. The WTG G_{ex} of Example 2 is not normalized. To illustrate the normalization step, we show the normalization of the production ρ_2, which is replaced by the following three productions:

$$q_{np} \xrightarrow{0.6} \mathrm{NP}(q_{dt}, q_n) \qquad q_{dt} \xrightarrow{1.0} \mathrm{DT}(q_t)$$
$$q_t \xrightarrow{1.0} \text{the} \ . \qquad \square$$

4 Weighted linear extended tree transducers

The model discussed in this contribution is an extension of the classical *top-down tree transducer*, which was introduced by Rounds (1970) and Thatcher (1970). Here we consider a weighted and extended variant that additionally has regular look-ahead. The weighted top-down tree transducer is discussed in (Fülöp and Vogler, 2009), and extended top-down tree transducers were studied in (Arnold and Dauchet, 1982; Knight and Graehl, 2005; Knight, 2007; Graehl et al., 2008; Graehl et al., 2009). The combination (weighted extended top-down tree transducer) was recently investigated by Fülöp et al. (2011), who also considered (weighted) regular look-ahead, which was first introduced by Engelfriet (1977) in the unweighted setting.

Definition 7. A *linear extended top-down tree transducer with full regular look-ahead* (l-XTOP$^{\mathrm{R}}_f$) is a system $(S, \Sigma, \Delta, s_0, G, R)$ where

- S is a finite set of *states*,
- Σ and Δ are alphabets of *input* and *output symbols*, respectively,
- $s_0 \in S$ is an *initial state*,
- $G = (Q, \Sigma, q_0, P)$ is a WTG, and
- R is a finite set of weighted *rules* of the form $\ell \xrightarrow{a}_\mu r$ where
  - $a \in A$ is the *rule weight*,
  - $\ell \in S[T_\Sigma(X)]$ is the linear *left-hand side*,
  - $\mu \colon \mathrm{var}(\ell) \to Q$ is the *look-ahead*, and
  - $r \in T_\Delta(S[\mathrm{var}(\ell)])$ is the linear *right-hand side*. □

In the following, let $M = (S, \Sigma, \Delta, s_0, G, R)$ be an l-XTOP$^{\mathrm{R}}_f$. We assume that the WTG G contains a state $\top$ such that $\mathrm{wt}_G(\top, t) = 1$ for every $t \in T_\Sigma$. In essence, this state represents the trivial look-ahead. If $\mu(x) = \top$ for every rule $\ell \xrightarrow{a}_\mu r \in R$ and $x \in \mathrm{var}(r)$ (respectively, $x \in \mathrm{var}(\ell)$), then M is an l-XTOP^{R} (respectively, l-XTOP). l-XTOP^{R} and l-XTOP coincide exactly with the models of Fülöp et al. (2011), and in the latter model we drop the look-ahead component μ and the WTG G completely.

Example 8. The rules of our running example l-XTOP M_{ex} (over the input and output alphabet Σ, which is also used by the WTG G_{ex} of Example 2) are displayed in Figure 3. □

Next, we present the semantics. Without loss of generality, we assume that we can distinguish states from input and output symbols (i.e., $S \cap (\Sigma \cup \Delta) = \emptyset$). A *sentential form* of M is a tree of $\mathrm{SF}(M) = T_\Delta(Q[T_\Sigma])$. Let $\rho = \ell \xrightarrow{a}_\mu r$ be a rule of R. Moreover, let $\xi, \zeta \in \mathrm{SF}(M)$ be sentential forms and $w \in \mathbb{N}^*$ be the lexicographically smallest position in $\mathrm{pos}_Q(\xi)$. We write $\xi \overset{b}{\Rightarrow}_{M,\rho} \zeta$ if there exists a substitution $\theta \colon X \to T_\Sigma$ such that

- $\xi = \xi[\ell\theta]_w$,
- $\zeta = \xi[r\theta]_w$, and
- $b = a \cdot \prod_{x \in \mathrm{var}(\ell)} \mathrm{wt}_G(\mu(x), \theta(x))$.

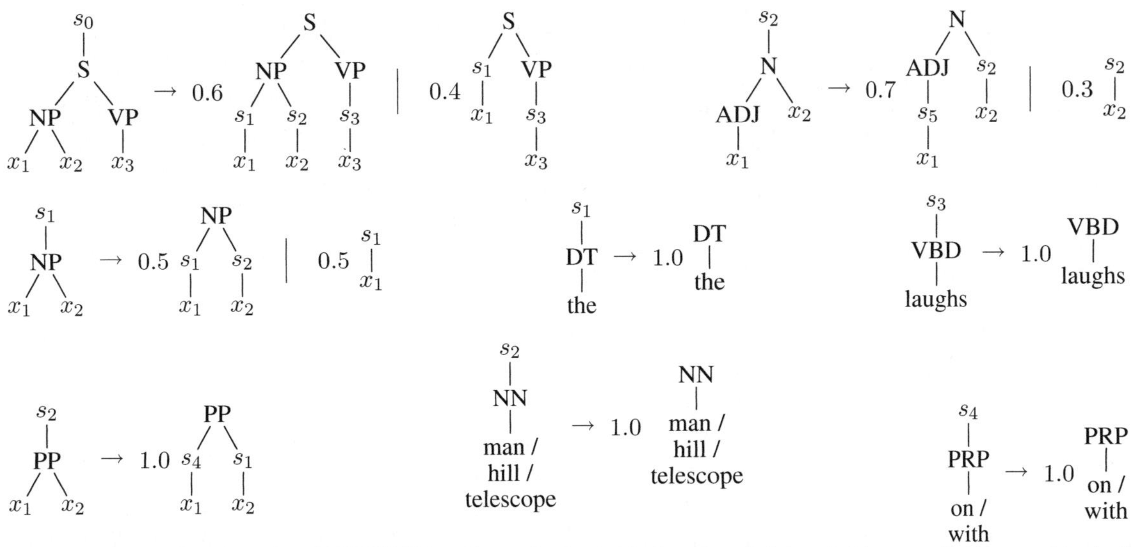

Figure 3: Example rules of an l-XTOP. We collapsed rules with the same left-hand side as well as several lexical items to save space.

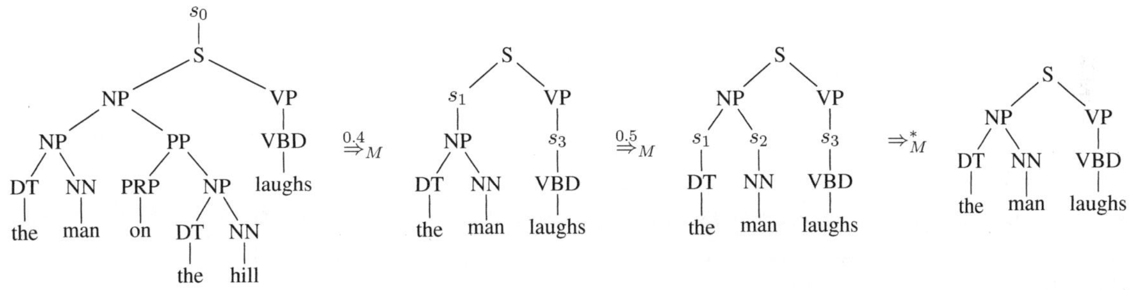

Figure 4: Derivation with weight $0.4 \cdot 0.5 \cdot 1.0$ (rules omitted).

The *tree transformation* τ_M *computed by* M is defined by

$$\tau_M(t, u) = \sum_{\substack{\rho_1,\dots,\rho_n \in R \\ s_0(t) \stackrel{a_1}{\Rightarrow}_{M,\rho_1} \cdots \stackrel{a_n}{\Rightarrow}_{M,\rho_n} u}} a_1 \cdot \ldots \cdot a_n$$

for every $t \in T_\Sigma$ and $u \in T_\Delta$.

Example 9. A sequence of derivation steps of the l-XTOP M_{ex} is illustrated in Figure 4. The transformation it computes is capable of deleting the PP child of every NP-node with probability 0.4 as well as deleting the ADJ child of every N-node with probability 0.3. □

A detailed exposition to unweighted l-XTOP^{R} is presented by Arnold and Dauchet (1982) and Graehl et al. (2009).

5 The construction

In this section, we present the main construction of this contribution, in which we will construct a WTG for the forward application of another WTG via an l-XTOP^{R}. Let us first introduce the main notions. Let $L \colon T_\Sigma \to A$ be a weighted forest and $\tau \colon T_\Sigma \times T_\Delta \to A$ be a weighted tree transformation. Then the forward application of L via τ yields the weighted forest $\tau(L) \colon T_\Delta \to A$ such that $(\tau(L))(u) = \sum_{t \in T_\Sigma} L(t) \cdot \tau(t, u)$ for every $u \in T_\Delta$. In other words, to compute the weight of u in $\tau(L)$, we consider all input trees t and multiply their weight in L with their translation weight to u. The sum of all those products yields the weight for u in $\tau(L)$. In the particular setting considered in this contribution, the weighted forest L is computed by a WTG and the weighted tree transformation τ is computed by an l-XTOP^{R}. The question is whether the resulting weighted forest $\tau(L)$ can be computed by a WTG.

Our approach to answer this question consists of three steps: (i) composition, (ii) normalization, and (iii) range projection, which we address in separate sections. Our input is

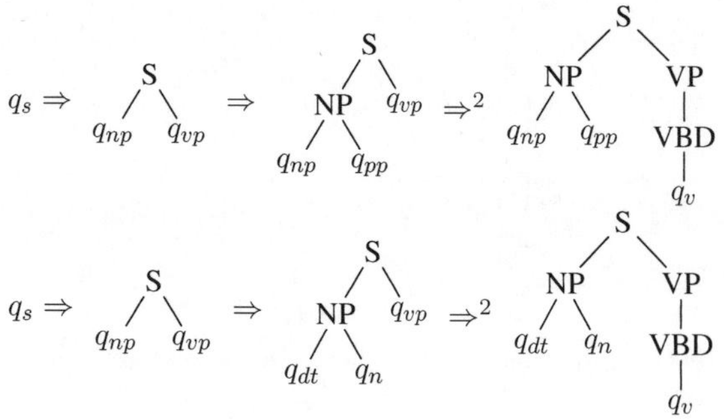

Figure 5: Two derivations (without production and grammar decoration) with weight 0.4 [top] and 0.6 [bottom] of the normalized version of the WTG G_{ex} (see Example 10).

the WTG $G' = (Q', \Sigma, q'_0, P')$, which computes the weighted forest $L = L_{G'}$, and the l-XTOP^{R} $M = (S, \Sigma, \Delta, s_0, G, R)$ with $G = (Q, \Sigma, q_0, P)$, which computes the weighted tree transformation $\tau = \tau_M$. Without loss of generality, we suppose that G and G' contain a special state $\top$ such that $\text{wt}_G(\top, t) = \text{wt}_{G'}(\top, t) = 1$ for all $t \in T_\Sigma$. Moreover, we assume that the WTG G' is in normal form. Finally, we assume that s_0 is separated, which means that the initial state of M does not occur in any right-hand side. Our example l-XTOP M_{ex} has this property. All these restrictions can be assumed without loss of generality. Finally, for every state $s \in S$, we let

$$R_s = \{\ell \xrightarrow{a}_\mu r \in R \mid \ell(\varepsilon) = s\} \ .$$

5.1 Composition

We combine the WTG G' and the l-XTOP^{R} M into a single l-XTOP$^{\text{R}}_f$ M' that computes

$$\tau_{M'}(t, u) = L_{G'}(t) \cdot \tau_M(t, u) = L(t) \cdot \tau(t, u)$$

for every $t \in T_\Sigma$ and $u \in T_\Delta$. To this end, we construct

$$M' = (S, \Sigma, \Delta, s_0, G \times G', (R \setminus R_{s_0}) \cup R')$$

such that $G \times G'$ is the classical product WTG [see Proposition 5.1 of (Berstel and Reutenauer, 1982)] and for every rule $\ell \xrightarrow{a}_\mu r$ in R_{s_0} and $\theta\colon \text{var}(\ell) \to Q'$, the rule

$$\ell \xrightarrow{a \cdot \text{wt}_{G'}(q'_0, \ell\theta)}_{\mu'} r$$

is in R', where $\mu'(x) = \langle \mu(x), \theta(x) \rangle$ for every $x \in \text{var}(\ell)$.

Example 10. Let us illustrate the construction on the WTG G_{ex} of Example 2 and the l-XTOP M_{ex} of Example 8. According to our assumptions, G_{ex} should first be normalized (see Theorem 5). We have two rules in R_{s_0} and they have the same left-hand side ℓ. It can be determined easily that $\text{wt}_{G'_{\text{ex}}}(q_s, \ell\theta) \neq 0$ only if

- $\theta(x_1)\theta(x_2)\theta(x_3) = q_{np}q_{pp}q_v$ or
- $\theta(x_1)\theta(x_2)\theta(x_3) = q_{dt}q_nq_v$.

Figure 5 shows the two corresponding derivations and their weights. Thus, the s_0-rules are replaced by the 4 rules displayed in Figure 6. □

Theorem 11. For every $t \in T_\Sigma$ and $u \in T_\Delta$, we have $\tau_{M'}(t, u) = L(t) \cdot \tau(t, u)$.

Proof. We prove an intermediate property for each derivation of M. Let

$$s_0(t) \overset{b_1}{\Rightarrow}_{M,\rho_1} \cdots \overset{b_n}{\Rightarrow}_{M,\rho_n} u$$

be a derivation of M. Let $\rho_1 = \ell \xrightarrow{a_1}_\mu r$ be the first rule, which trivially must be in R_{s_0}. Then for every $\theta\colon \text{var}(\ell) \to Q'$, there exists a derivation

$$s_0(t) \overset{c_1}{\Rightarrow}_{M',\rho'_1} \xi_2 \overset{b_2}{\Rightarrow}_{M',\rho_2} \cdots \overset{b_n}{\Rightarrow}_{M',\rho_n} u$$

in M' such that

$$c_1 = b_1 \cdot \text{wt}_{G'}(q'_0, \ell\theta) \cdot \prod_{x \in \text{var}(\ell)} \text{wt}_{G'}(\theta(x), \theta'(x)) \ ,$$

where $\theta'\colon \text{var}(\ell) \to T_\Sigma$ is such that $t = \ell\theta'$. Since we sum over all such derivations and

$$\sum_{\theta\colon \text{var}(\ell) \to Q'} \text{wt}_{G'}(q'_0, \ell\theta) \cdot \prod_{x \in \text{var}(\ell)} \text{wt}_{G'}(\theta(x), \theta'(x))$$
$$= \text{wt}_{G'}(q'_0, t) = L_{G'}(t)$$

by a straightforward extension of Lemma 4.1.8 of (Borchardt, 2005), we obtain that the derivations in M' sum to $L_{G'}(t) \cdot b_1 \cdot \ldots \cdot b_n$ as desired. The main property follows trivially from the intermediate result. □

5.2 Normalization

Currently, the weights of the input WTG are only on the initial rules and in its look-ahead. Next, we use essentially the same method as in the previous section to remove the look-ahead from all variables that are not deleted. Let $M' = (S, \Sigma, \Delta, s_0, G \times G', R)$ be the l-XTOP$^{\text{R}}_f$ constructed in the previous section and

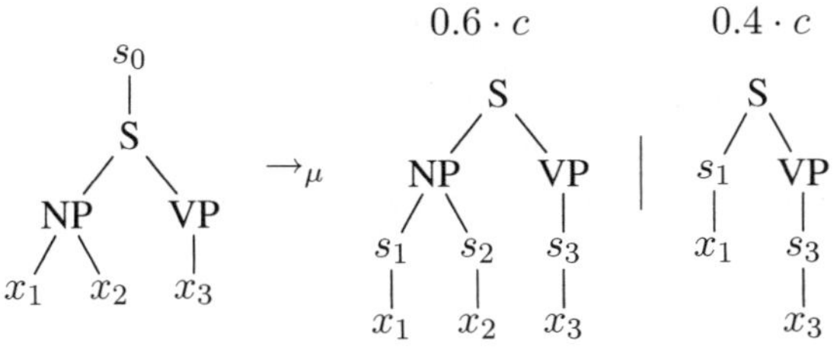

Figure 6: 4 new l-XTOP$^{\text{R}}_f$ rules, where μ and c are either (i) $\mu(x_1)\mu(x_2)\mu(x_3) = q_{np}q_{pp}q_v$ and $c = 0.4$ or (ii) $\mu(x_1)\mu(x_2)\mu(x_3) = q_{dt}q_nq_v$ and $c = 0.6$ (see Example 10).

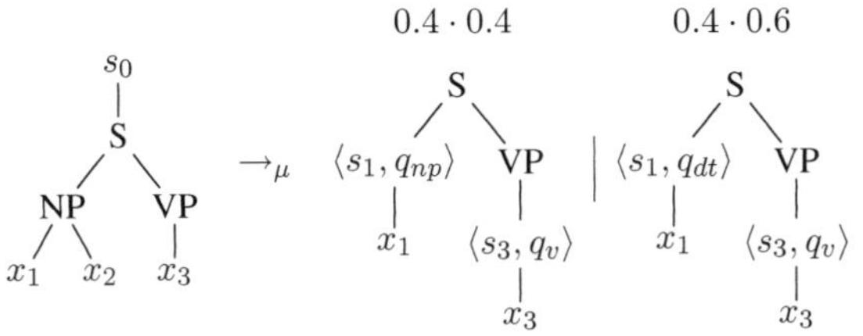

Figure 7: New l-XTOP^{R} rules, where $\mu(x_2) = q_{pp}$ [left] and $\mu(x_2) = q_n$ [right] (see Figure 6).

$\rho = \ell \xrightarrow{a}_\mu r \in R$ be a rule with $\mu(x) = \langle \top, q' \rangle$ for some $q' \in Q' \setminus \{\top\}$ and $x \in \text{var}(r)$. Note that $\mu(x) = \langle \top, q' \rangle$ for some $q' \in Q'$ for all $x \in \text{var}(r)$ since M is an l-XTOP^{R}. Then we construct the l-XTOP$^{\text{R}}_f$ M''

$$(S \cup S \times Q', \Sigma, \Delta, s_0, G \times G', (R \setminus \{\rho\}) \cup R')$$

such that R' contains the rule $\ell \xrightarrow{a}_{\mu'} r'$, where

$$\mu'(x') = \begin{cases} \langle \top, \top \rangle & \text{if } x = x' \\ \mu(x') & \text{otherwise} \end{cases}$$

for all $x' \in \text{var}(\ell)$ and r' is obtained from r by replacing the subtree $s(x)$ with $s \in S$ by $\langle s, q' \rangle(x)$. Additionally, for every rule $\ell'' \xrightarrow{a''}_{\mu''} r''$ in R_s and $\theta \colon \text{var}(\ell'') \to Q'$, the rule

$$\ell'' \xrightarrow{a'' \cdot \text{wt}_{G'}(q', \ell''\theta)}_{\mu'''} r''$$

is in R', where $\mu'''(x) = \langle \mu''(x), \theta(x) \rangle$ for every $x \in \text{var}(\ell)$. This procedure is iterated until we obtain an l-XTOP^{R} M''. Clearly, the iteration must terminate since we do not change the rule shape, which yields that the size of the potential rule set is bounded.

Theorem 12. The l-XTOP^{R} M'' and the l-XTOP$^{\text{R}}_f$ M' are equivalent.

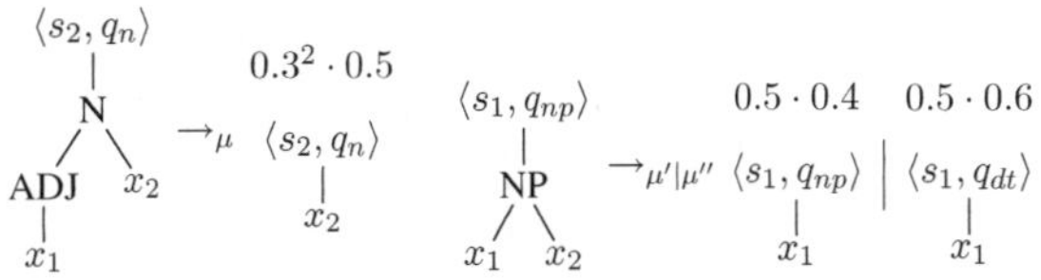

Figure 8: New l-XTOP^{R} rules, where $\mu(x_1)$ is either q_{old} or q_{young}, $\mu'(x_2) = q_{pp}$, and $\mu''(x_2) = q_n$.

Proof. It can be proved that the l-XTOP$^{\text{R}}_f$ constructed after each iteration is equivalent to its input l-XTOP$^{\text{R}}_f$ in the same fashion as in Theorem 11 with the only difference that the rule replacement now occurs anywhere in the derivation (not necessarily at the beginning) and potentially several times. Consequently, the finally obtained l-XTOP^{R} M'' is equivalent to M'. □

Example 13. Let us reconsider the l-XTOP$^{\text{R}}_f$ constructed in the previous section and apply the normalization step. The interesting rules (i.e., those rules $l \xrightarrow{a}_\mu r$ where $\text{var}(r) \neq \text{var}(l)$) are displayed in Figures 7 and 8. □

5.3 Range projection

We now have an l-XTOP^{R} M'' with rules R'' computing $\tau_{M''}(t, u) = L(t) \cdot \tau(t, u)$. In the final step, we simply disregard the input and project to the output. Formally, we want to construct a WTG G'' such that

$$L_{G''}(u) = \sum_{t \in T_\Sigma} \tau_{M''}(t, u) = \sum_{t \in T_\Sigma} L(t) \cdot \tau(t, u)$$

for every $u \in T_\Delta$. Let us suppose that $\overline{G}$ is the WTG inside M''. Recall that the *inside weight* of state $q \in Q$ is

$$\text{in}_{\overline{G}}(q) = \sum_{t \in T_\Sigma} \text{wt}_{\overline{G}}(q, t) \ .$$

We construct the WTG

$$G'' = (S \cup S \times Q', \Delta, s_0, P'')$$

such that $\ell(\varepsilon) \xrightarrow{c} r'$ is in P'' for every rule $\ell \xrightarrow{a}_\mu r \in R''$, where

$$c = a \cdot \prod_{x \in \text{var}(\ell) \setminus \text{var}(r)} \text{in}_{\overline{G}}(\mu(x))$$

and r' is obtained from r by removing the variables of X. If the same production is constructed from several rules, then we add the weights. Note that the WTG G'' can be effectively computed if $\text{in}_{\overline{G}}(q)$ is computable for every state q.

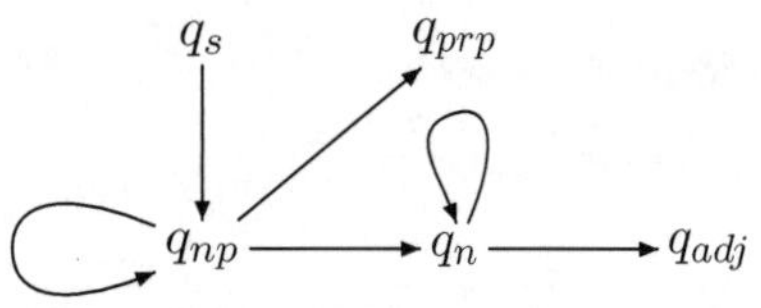

Figure 9: Dependency graph of the WTG G_{ex}.

Theorem 14. For every $u \in T_\Delta$, we have

$$L_{G''}(u) = \sum_{t \in T_\Sigma} L(t) \cdot \tau(t, u) = (\tau(L))(u) \ .$$

□

Example 15. The WTG productions for the rules of Figures 7 and 8 are

$$s_0 \overset{0.4 \cdot 0.4}{\to} \text{S}(\langle s_1, q_{np}\rangle, \text{VP}(\langle s_3, q_v\rangle))$$
$$s_0 \overset{0.4 \cdot 0.6}{\to} \text{S}(\langle s_1, q_{dt}\rangle, \text{VP}(\langle s_3, q_v\rangle))$$
$$\langle s_2, q_n\rangle \overset{0.3 \cdot 0.3}{\to} \langle s_2, q_n\rangle$$
$$\langle s_1, q_{np}\rangle \overset{0.5 \cdot 0.4}{\to} \langle s_1, q_{np}\rangle$$
$$\langle s_1, q_{np}\rangle \overset{0.5 \cdot 0.6}{\to} \langle s_1, q_{dt}\rangle \ .$$

Note that all inside weights are 1 in our example. The first production uses the inside weight of q_{pp}, whereas the second production uses the inside weight of q_n. Note that the third production can be constructed twice. □

6 Computation of inside weights

In this section, we address how to effectively compute the inside weight for every state. If the WTG $G = (Q, \Sigma, q_0, P)$ permits only finitely many derivations, then for every $q \in Q$, the inside weight $\text{in}_G(q)$ can be computed according to Definition 4 because $\text{wt}_G(q, t) = 0$ for almost all $t \in T_\Sigma$. If P contains (useful) recursive rules, then this approach does not work anymore. Our WTG G_{ex} of Example 2 has the following two recursive rules:

$$q_{np} \overset{0.4}{\to} \text{NP}(q_{np}, \text{PP}(q_{prp}, q_{np})) \qquad (\rho_4)$$
$$q_n \overset{0.3}{\to} \text{N}(q_{adj}, q_n) \ . \qquad (\rho_5)$$

The dependency graph of G_{ex}, which is shown in Figure 9, has cycles, which yields that G_{ex} permits infinitely many derivations. Due to the completeness of the semiring, even the infinite sum of Definition 4 is well-defined, but we still have to compute it. We will present two simple methods to achieve this: (a) an analytic method and (b) an approximation in the next sections.

6.1 Analytic computation

In simple cases we can compute the inside weight using the stars a^*, which we defined in Section 2. Let us first list some interesting countably complete semirings for NLP applications and their corresponding stars.

- *Probabilities:* $(\mathbb{R}^\infty_{\geq 0}, +, \cdot, 0, 1)$ where $\mathbb{R}^\infty_{\geq 0}$ contains all nonnegative real numbers and ∞, which is bigger than every real number. For every $a \in \mathbb{R}^\infty_{\geq 0}$ we have

$$a^* = \begin{cases} \frac{1}{1-a} & \text{if } 0 \leq a < 1 \\ \infty & \text{otherwise} \end{cases}$$

- VITERBI*:* $([0, 1], \max, \cdot, 0, 1)$ where $[0, 1]$ is the (inclusive) interval of real numbers between 0 and 1. For every $0 \leq a \leq 1$ we have $a^* = 1$.

- *Tropical:* $(\mathbb{R}^\infty_{\geq 0}, \min, +, \infty, 0)$ where $a^* = 0$ for every $a \in \mathbb{R}^\infty_{\geq 0}$.

- *Tree unification:* $(2^{T_\Sigma(X_1)}, \cup, \sqcup, \emptyset, \{x_1\})$ where $2^{T_\Sigma(X_1)} = \{L \mid L \subseteq T_\Sigma(X_1)\}$ and $\sqcup$ is unification (where different occurrences of x_1 can be replaced differently) extended to sets as usual. For every $L \subseteq T_\Sigma(X_k)$ we have $L^* = \{x_1\} \cup (L \sqcup L)$.

We can always try to develop a regular expression (Fülöp and Vogler, 2009) for the weighted forest recognized by a certain state, in which we then can drop the actual trees and only compute with the weights. This is particularly easy if our WTG has only left- or right-recursive productions because in this case we obtain classical regular expressions (for strings). Let us consider production ρ_5. It is right-recursive. On the string level, we obtain the following unweighted regular expression for the string language generated by q_n:

$$L(q_{adj})^*(\text{man} \mid \text{hill} \mid \text{telescope})$$

where $L(q_{adj}) = \{\text{old}, \text{young}\}$ is the set of strings generated by q_{adj}. Correspondingly, we can derive the inside weight by replacing the generated string with the weights used to derive them. For example, the production ρ_5, which generates the state q_{adj}, has weight 0.3. We obtain the expression

$$\text{in}_G(q_n) = (0.3 \cdot \text{in}_G(q_{adj}))^* \cdot (0.3 + 0.2 + 0.2) \ .$$

Example 16. If we calculate in the probability semiring and $\text{in}_G(q_{adj}) = 1$, then

$$\text{in}_G(q_n) = \frac{1}{1-0.3} \cdot (0.3 + 0.2 + 0.2) = 1 \ ,$$

as expected (since our productions induce a probability distribution on all trees generated from each state). □

Example 17. If we calculate in the *tropical semiring*, then we obtain

$$\text{in}_G(q_n) = \min(0.3, 0.2, 0.2) = 0.2 \ . \qquad \square$$

It should be stressed that this method only allows us to compute $\text{in}_G(q)$ in very simple cases (e.g., WTG containing only left- or right-recursive productions). The production ρ_4 has a more complicated recursion, so this simple method cannot be used for our full example WTG.

However, for extremal semirings the inside weight always coincides with a particular derivation. Let us also recall this result. The semiring is *extremal* if $a + a' \in \{a, a'\}$ for all $a, a' \in A$. The VITERBI and the tropical semiring are extremal. Recall that

$$\begin{aligned}\text{in}_G(q) &= \sum_{t \in T_\Sigma} \text{wt}_G(q, t) \\ &= \sum_{t \in T_\Sigma} \sum_{\substack{\rho_1, \dots, \rho_n \in P \\ q \Rightarrow_G^{\rho_1} \cdots \Rightarrow_G^{\rho_n} t}} \text{wt}_G(\rho_1 \cdots \rho_n) \ ,\end{aligned}$$

which yields that $\text{in}_G(q)$ coincides with the derivation weight $\text{wt}_G(\rho_1 \cdots \rho_n)$ of some derivation $q \Rightarrow_G^{\rho_1} \cdots \Rightarrow_G^{\rho_n} t$ for some $t \in T_\Sigma$. In the VITERBI semiring this is the highest scoring derivation and in the tropical semiring it is the lowest scoring derivation (mind that in the VITERBI semiring the production weights are multiplied in a derivation, whereas they are added in the tropical semiring). There are efficient algorithms (Viterbi, 1967) that compute those derivations and their weights.

6.2 Numerical Approximation

Next, we show how to obtain a numerical approximation of the inside weights (up to any desired precision) in the probability semiring, which is the most important of all semirings discussed here. A similar approach was used by Stolcke (1995) for context-free grammars. To keep the presentation simple, let us suppose that $G = (Q, \Sigma, q_0, P)$ is in normal form (see Theorem 5). The method works just as well in the general case.

We first observe an important property of the inside weights. For every state $q \in Q$

$$\text{in}_G(q) = \sum_{q \xrightarrow{a} \sigma(q_1, \dots, q_n) \in P} a \cdot \text{in}_G(q_1) \cdot \ldots \cdot \text{in}_G(q_n) \ ,$$

which can trivially be understood as a system of equations (where each $\text{in}_G(q)$ with $q \in Q$ is a variable). Since there is one such equation for each variable $\text{in}_G(q)$ with $q \in Q$, we have a system of $|Q|$ non-linear polynomial equations in $|Q|$ variables.

Several methods to solve non-linear systems of equations are known in the numerical calculus literature. For example, the NEWTON-RAPHSON method allows us to iteratively compute the roots of any differentiable real-valued function, which can be used to solve our system of equations because we can compute the JACOBI matrix for our system of equations easily. Given a good starting point, the NEWTON-RAPHSON method assures quadratic convergence to a root. A good starting point can be obtained, for example, by bisection (Corliss, 1977). Another popular root-finding approximation is described by Brent (1973).

Example 18. For the WTG of Example 2 we obtain the following system of equations:

$$\begin{aligned}\text{in}_G(q_s) &= 1.0 \cdot \text{in}_G(q_{np}) \\ \text{in}_G(q_{np}) &= 0.4 \cdot \text{in}_G(q_{np}) \cdot \text{in}_G(q_{prp}) \cdot \text{in}_G(q_{np}) \\ &\quad + 0.6 \cdot \text{in}_G(q_n) \\ \text{in}_G(q_n) &= 0.3 \cdot \text{in}_G(q_{adj}) \cdot \text{in}_G(q_n) \\ &\quad + 0.3 + 0.2 + 0.2 \\ \text{in}_G(q_{adj}) &= 0.5 + 0.5 \\ \text{in}_G(q_{prp}) &= 0.5 + 0.5 \ .\end{aligned}$$

Together with $\text{in}_G(q_n) = 1$, which we already calculated in Example 16, the only interesting value is

$$\text{in}_G(q_s) = \text{in}_G(q_{np}) = 0.4 \cdot \text{in}_G(q_{np})^2 + 0.6 \ ,$$

which yields the roots $\text{in}_G(q_{np}) = 1$ and $\text{in}_G(q_{np}) = 1.5$. The former is the desired solution. As before, this is the expected solution. □

References

Athanasios Alexandrakis and Symeon Bozapalidis. 1987. Weighted grammars and Kleene's theorem. *Inf. Process. Lett.*, 24(1):1–4.

André Arnold and Max Dauchet. 1982. Morphismes et bimorphismes d'arbres. *Theoret. Comput. Sci.*, 20(1):33–93.

Jean Berstel and Christophe Reutenauer. 1982. Recognizable formal power series on trees. *Theoret. Comput. Sci.*, 18(2):115–148.

Björn Borchardt. 2005. *The Theory of Recognizable Tree Series*. Ph.D. thesis, Technische Universität Dresden.

Richard P. Brent. 1973. *Algorithms for Minimization without Derivatives*. Series in Automatic Computation. Prentice Hall, Englewood Cliffs, NJ, USA.

George Corliss. 1977. Which root does the bisection algorithm find? *SIAM Review*, 19(2):325–327.

Samuel Eilenberg. 1974. *Automata, Languages, and Machines — Volume A*, volume 59 of *Pure and Applied Math.* Academic Press.

Joost Engelfriet. 1975. Bottom-up and top-down tree transformations — a comparison. *Math. Systems Theory*, 9(3):198–231.

Joost Engelfriet. 1977. Top-down tree transducers with regular look-ahead. *Math. Systems Theory*, 10(1):289–303.

Zoltán Fülöp and Heiko Vogler. 2009. Weighted tree automata and tree transducers. In Manfred Droste, Werner Kuich, and Heiko Vogler, editors, *Handbook of Weighted Automata*, EATCS Monographs on Theoret. Comput. Sci., chapter 9, pages 313–403. Springer.

Zoltán Fülöp, Andreas Maletti, and Heiko Vogler. 2010. Preservation of recognizability for synchronous tree substitution grammars. In *Proc. 1st Workshop Applications of Tree Automata in Natural Language Processing*, pages 1–9. Association for Computational Linguistics.

Zoltán Fülöp, Andreas Maletti, and Heiko Vogler. 2011. Weighted extended tree transducers. *Fundam. Inform.*, 111(2):163–202.

Jonathan S. Golan. 1999. *Semirings and their Applications*. Kluwer Academic, Dordrecht.

Jonathan Graehl, Kevin Knight, and Jonathan May. 2008. Training tree transducers. *Comput. Linguist.*, 34(3):391–427.

Jonathan Graehl, Mark Hopkins, Kevin Knight, and Andreas Maletti. 2009. The power of extended top-down tree transducers. *SIAM J. Comput.*, 39(2):410–430.

Udo Hebisch and Hanns J. Weinert. 1998. *Semirings — Algebraic Theory and Applications in Computer Science*. World Scientific.

Georg Karner. 2004. Continuous monoids and semirings. *Theoret. Comput. Sci.*, 318(3):355–372.

Kevin Knight and Jonathan Graehl. 2005. An overview of probabilistic tree transducers for natural language processing. In *Proc. 6th Int. Conf. Computational Linguistics and Intelligent Text Processing*, volume 3406 of LNCS, pages 1–24. Springer.

Kevin Knight. 2007. Capturing practical natural language transformations. *Machine Translation*, 21(2):121–133.

Karim Lari and Steve J. Young. 1990. The estimation of stochastic context-free grammars using the inside-outside algorithm. *Computer Speech and Language*, 4(1):35–56.

Andreas Maletti and Giorgio Satta. 2009. Parsing algorithms based on tree automata. In *Proc. 11th Int. Workshop Parsing Technologies*, pages 1–12. Association for Computational Linguistics.

Haitao Mi, Liang Huang, and Qun Liu. 2008. Forest-based translation. In *Proc. 46th Ann. Meeting of the ACL*, pages 192–199. Association for Computational Linguistics.

William C. Rounds. 1970. Mappings and grammars on trees. *Math. Systems Theory*, 4(3):257–287.

Andreas Stolcke. 1995. An efficient probabilistic context-free parsing algorithm that computes prefix probabilities. *Comput. Linguist.*, 21(2):165–201.

James W. Thatcher. 1970. Generalized^2 sequential machine maps. *J. Comput. System Sci.*, 4(4):339–367.

Andrew J. Viterbi. 1967. Error bounds for convolutional codes and an asymptotically optimum decoding algorithm. *IEEE Trans. Inform. Theory*, 13(2):260–269.

Deciding the Twins Property for Weighted Tree Automata over Extremal Semifields

Matthias Büchse and **Anja Fischer**
Department of Computer Science
Technische Universität Dresden
01062 Dresden, Germany
Matthias.Buechse@tu-dresden.de

Abstract

It has remained an open question whether the twins property for weighted tree automata is decidable. This property is crucial for determinizing such an automaton, and it has been argued that determinization improves the output of parsers and translation systems. We show that the twins property for weighted tree automata over extremal semifields is decidable.

1 Introduction

In natural-language processing (NLP), language and translation are often modeled using some kind of grammar, automaton or transducer, such as a probabilistic context-free grammar, a synchronous context-free grammar, a weighted tree automaton, or a tree transducer, among others (May and Knight, 2006; Petrov et al., 2006; Chiang, 2007; Graehl, Knight and May, 2008; Zhang et al., 2008; Pauls and Klein, 2009). In statistical NLP, the structure of the grammar is extracted heuristically from a large corpus of example sentences or sentence pairs, and the rule weights are estimated using methods from statistics or machine learning.

In general, a grammar such as those named above will be *ambiguous*, i.e., offering several ways of deriving the same object (sentence or sentence pair). While the derivation of an object is crucial to the intrinsics of a system, it is neither relevant to the user nor observed in the corpus. Hence, we speak of *spurious ambiguity* (Li, Eisner and Khudanpur, 2009).

As a consequence, the true importance of an object can only be assessed by aggregating all its derivations. Unfortunately, this proves computationally intractable in almost all cases: for instance, finding the best string of a probabilistic regular grammar is NP hard (Sima'an, 1996; Casacuberta and de la Higuera, 2000). Finding the best derivation, on the other hand, is possible in polynomial time (Eppstein, 1998; Huang and Chiang, 2005), and thus, most NLP systems approximate the importance of an object by its best derivation (Li, Eisner and Khudanpur, 2009).

There is, however, a line of research that deals with the costly aggregating approach, and it is closely related to determinization techniques from automata theory.

For instance, May and Knight (2006) argue that the output of a parser or syntax-based translation system can be represented by a weighted tree automaton (wta), which assigns a weight to each parse tree. Under some circumstances, the wta can be determinized, yielding an equivalent, but unambiguous wta, which offers at most one derivation for each object. Then the weight of an object is equal to the weight of its derivation, and the aforementioned polynomial-time algorithms deliver exact results.

The caveat of the determinization approach is that deterministic weighted automata are strictly less powerful than their general counterparts, i.e., not every automaton can be determinized. Büchse, May and Vogler (2010) give a review of known sufficient conditions under which determinization is possible. One of these conditions requires that (i) the weights are calculated in an extremal semiring, (ii) there is a maximal factorization, and (iii) the wta has the twins property.[1]

[1] Items (i) and (iii) guarantee that the wta only computes weight vectors that are scalar multiples of a finite number

Regarding (i), we note that in an extremal semiring the weight of a parse tree is equal to the weight of its best derivation. It follows that, while the determinized wta will have at most one derivation per parse tree, its weight will be the weight of the best derivation of the original wta. The benefit of determinization reduces to removing superfluous derivations from the list of best derivations.

Regarding (ii), the factorization is used in the determinization construction to distribute the weight computation in the determinized automaton between its transition weights and its state behavior. A maximal factorization exists for every zero-sum free semifield.

Regarding (iii), the question whether the twins property is decidable has remained open for a long time, until Kirsten (2012)[2] gave an affirmative answer for a particular case: weighted string automata over the tropical semiring. He also showed that the decision problem is PSPACE-complete.

In this paper, we close one remaining gap by adapting and generalizing Kirsten's proof: we show that the twins property is decidable for wta over extremal semifields (Theorem 3.1). We proceed by recalling the concepts related to determinizing wta, such as ranked trees, semirings, factorizations, wta themselves, and the twins property (Sec. 2). Then we show our main theorem, including two decision algorithms (Sec. 3). Finally, we conclude the paper with a discussion and some open questions (Sec. 4).

2 Preliminaries

2.1 Ranked Trees

A *ranked alphabet* is a tuple (Σ, rk) where Σ is an alphabet, i.e., a finite set, and $rk\colon \Sigma \to \mathbb{N}$ assigns an *arity* to every symbol $\sigma \in \Sigma$. Throughout this paper we will identify (Σ, rk) with Σ. For every $k \in \mathbb{N}$ the set $\Sigma^{(k)} = \{\sigma \in \Sigma \mid rk(\sigma) = k\}$ contains all symbols of arity k.

Let H be a set and Σ a ranked alphabet. The set $T_\Sigma(H)$ of *trees over* Σ *indexed by* H is defined inductively as the smallest set T such that: (i) $H \subseteq T$ and (ii) $\sigma(\xi_1, \ldots, \xi_k) \in T$ for every $k \in \mathbb{N}$, $\sigma \in \Sigma^{(k)}$, and $\xi_1, \ldots, \xi_k \in T$. We write T_Σ instead of $T_\Sigma(\emptyset)$.

For every $\xi \in T_\Sigma(H)$, we define the set $\mathrm{pos}(\xi) \subseteq \mathbb{N}^*$ of *positions of* ξ by

(i) if $\xi \in H$, then $\mathrm{pos}(\xi) = \{\varepsilon\}$;

(ii) if $\xi = \sigma(\xi_1, \ldots, \xi_k)$, then $\mathrm{pos}(\xi) = \{\varepsilon\} \cup \{i \cdot w \mid i \in \{1, \ldots, k\}, w \in \mathrm{pos}(\xi_i)\}$.

The mapping $\mathrm{ht}\colon T_\Sigma(H) \to \mathbb{N}$ maps each tree ξ to its *height*, i.e., the length of a longest position of ξ. We denote the *label of* ξ *at position* w by $\xi(w)$, the *subtree of* ξ *rooted at* w by $\xi|_w$, and the tree obtained by *replacing the subtree of* ξ *rooted at position* w *with* ξ', $\xi' \in T_\Sigma(H)$, by $\xi[\xi']_w$.

A Σ-*context* is a tree in $T_\Sigma(\{z\})$ that contains exactly one occurrence of the special symbol z. The set of all Σ-contexts is denoted by C_Σ. Let $\xi \in T_\Sigma \cup C_\Sigma$ and $\zeta \in C_\Sigma$. Then the *concatenation of* ξ *and* ζ, denoted by $\xi \cdot \zeta$, is obtained from ζ by replacing the leaf z by ξ. If $\xi \in T_\Sigma$, then so is $\xi \cdot \zeta$, and likewise for $\xi \in C_\Sigma$.

2.2 Semirings

A *semiring* (Hebisch and Weinert, 1998; Golan, 1999) is a quintuple $\mathcal{S} = (S, +, \cdot, 0, 1)$ where S is a set, $+$ and $\cdot$ are binary, associative operations on S, called *addition* and *multiplication*, respectively, $+$ is commutative, $\cdot$ distributes over $+$ from both sides, 0 and 1 are elements of S, 0 is neutral with respect to $+$, 1 is neutral with respect to $\cdot$, and 0 is absorbing with respect to $\cdot$ (i.e., $s \cdot 0 = 0 = 0 \cdot s$).

Let $\mathcal{S} = (S, +, \cdot, 0, 1)$ be a semiring. In notation, we will identify $\mathcal{S}$ with S. We call S *commutative* if the multiplication is commutative; a *semifield* if it is commutative and for every $a \in S \setminus \{0\}$ there is an $a^{-1} \in S$ such that $a \cdot a^{-1} = 1$; *zero-sum free* if $a + b = 0$ implies $a = b = 0$; *zero-divisor free* if $a \cdot b = 0$ implies $a = 0$ or $b = 0$; and *extremal* (Mahr, 1984) if $a + b \in \{a, b\}$. We note that every extremal semiring is also zero-sum free and every semifield is zero-divisor free.

Example 2.1 We present four examples of semirings. The *Boolean semiring* $\mathbb{B} = (\{0, 1\}, \vee, \wedge, 0, 1)$, with disjunction and conjunction, is an extremal semifield. The *formal-language semiring* $(\mathcal{P}(\Sigma^*), \cup, \cdot, \emptyset, \{\varepsilon\})$ over an alphabet Σ, with union and language concatenation, is neither commutative nor extremal, but zero-divisor free and zero-sum free. The *tropical semiring* $(\mathbb{R} \cup \{\infty\}, \min, +, \infty, 0)$, with minimum and conventional addition, is

of vectors corresponding to a set of height-bounded trees, while Item (ii) ensures that the latter vectors suffice as the states of the constructed deterministic wta; cf. (Büchse, May and Vogler, 2010, Lm. 5.9 and Lm. 5.8, respectively).

[2] A manuscript with the same content has been available on Daniel Kirsten's website for a year from Sept. 2010 on.

an extremal semifield. The *Viterbi semiring* $([0,1], \max, \cdot, 0, 1)$ is a commutative, extremal, zero-divisor-free semiring, but not a semifield. □

Let Q be a set. The set S^Q contains all mappings $u\colon Q \to S$, or, equivalently, all Q-vectors over S. Instead of $u(q)$ we also write u_q to denote the q-component of a vector $u \in S^Q$. The Q-vector mapping every q to 0 is denoted by $\tilde{0}$. For every $q \in Q$ we define $e_q \in S^Q$ such that $(e_q)_q = 1$, and $(e_q)_p = 0$ for every $p \neq q$.

2.3 Factorizations

We use the notion of a factorization as defined in (Kirsten and Mäurer, 2005).

Let Q be a nonempty finite set. A pair (f, g) is called a *factorization of dimension* Q if $f\colon S^Q \setminus \{\tilde{0}\} \to S^Q$, $g\colon S^Q \setminus \{\tilde{0}\} \to S$, and $u = g(u) \cdot f(u)$ for every $u \in S^Q \setminus \{\tilde{0}\}$. A factorization (f, g) is called *maximal* if for every $u \in S^Q$ and $a \in S$, we have that $a \cdot u \neq \tilde{0}$ implies $f(a \cdot u) = f(u)$.

Example 2.2 Let Q be a nonempty finite set. We show three factorizations of dimension Q.

If S is an arbitrary semiring, $g(u) = 1$ and $f(u) = u$ constitute the *trivial factorization.* It is not maximal in general.

If S is a zero-sum free semifield, such as the tropical semiring or the semifield of non-negative reals, then $g(u) = \sum_{q \in Q} u_q$ and $f(u) = \frac{1}{g(u)} \cdot u$ constitute a factorization (Büchse, May and Vogler, 2010, Lemma 4.2). It is maximal: $f(a \cdot u) = \frac{1}{g(a \cdot u)} \cdot (a \cdot u) = \frac{1}{a \cdot g(u)} \cdot a \cdot u = f(u)$.

As shown in (Büchse, May and Vogler, 2010, Lemma 4.4) a maximal factorization only exists if S is zero-divisor free or $|Q| = 1$.

2.4 Weighted Tree Automata

A weighted tree automaton (Ésik and Kuich, 2003) is a finite-state machine that represents a *weighted tree language*, i.e., a mapping $\varphi\colon T_\Sigma \to S$. It assigns a weight to every tree based on weighted transitions.

Formally, a *weighted tree automaton (wta)* is a tuple $\mathcal{A} = (Q, \Sigma, S, \delta, \nu)$ such that Q is a nonempty finite set (of *states*), Σ is a ranked alphabet, S is a semiring, δ is the *transition mapping*, mapping *transitions* $(q_1 \cdots q_k, \sigma, q)$ into S where $q_1, \ldots, q_k, q \in Q$ and $\sigma \in \Sigma^{(k)}$, and $\nu \in S^Q$ maps every state to its *root weight.*

A wta $\mathcal{A}$ is *bottom-up deterministic* if for every $(q_1 \cdots q_k, \sigma)$, there is at most one q such that $\delta(q_1 \cdots q_k, \sigma, q) \neq 0$.

Example 2.3 Let $\mathcal{A} = (Q, \Sigma, S, \delta, \nu)$ be the wta where $\Sigma = \{\alpha^{(0)}, \gamma^{(1)}, \sigma^{(2)}\}$, S is the arctic semiring $(\mathbb{N} \cup \{-\infty\}, \max, +, -\infty, 0)$, δ is given by the directed functional hypergraph in Fig. 1, and $\nu = (0, -\infty)$. Each node in the hypergraph (drawn as circle) corresponds to a state, and each hyperedge (drawn as box with arbitrarily many ingoing arcs and exactly one outgoing arc) represents a weighted transition. Ingoing arcs of a hyperedge are meant to be read counter-clockwise, starting from the outgoing arc. The final weight 0 of q_1 is indicated by an additional arc. Transitions not shown have the weight $-\infty$. □

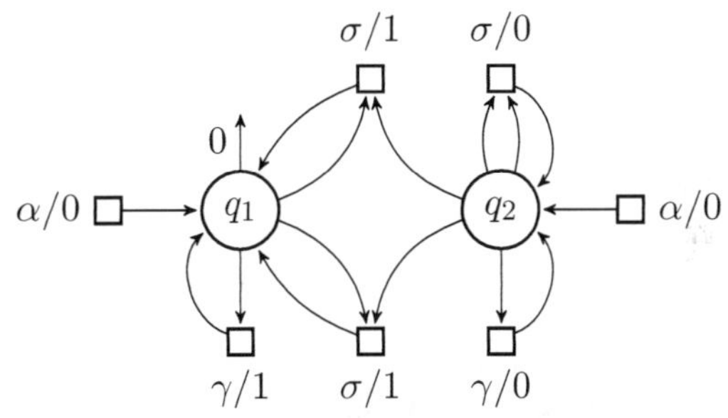

Figure 1: Hypergraph representation of wta $\mathcal{A}$.

Typically, wta are given initial-algebra semantics (Goguen et al., 1977). In this paper, we use the equivalent run semantics (Fülöp and Vogler, 2009, Sec. 3.2) as it constitutes the basis for our proofs. In this setting, every node of a given tree is decorated with a state; this decoration is called a *run*. The label of a node, its state, and the states of its successors comprise a transition. The weight of a run is given by the product of the weights of all these transitions (under δ), calculated in the semiring S. Roughly speaking, the weight of a tree is then the sum of the weights of all runs on that tree, again calculated in S.

Now we formalize the notions of a run and its weight. For our proofs, we will need runs and their weights to be as easily composable and decomposable as trees and contexts. Therefore, we will consider trees indexed by semiring elements and even Q-vectors over S. Let H be a set, $\xi \in T_\Sigma(H)$, and $q \in Q$. The *set* $R^q_{\mathcal{A}}(\xi)$ *of all runs on* ξ *that end in state* q *at the root of* ξ is

$$R^q_{\mathcal{A}}(\xi) = \{(\xi, \kappa) \mid \kappa\colon \mathrm{pos}(\xi) \to Q, \kappa(\varepsilon) = q\} .$$

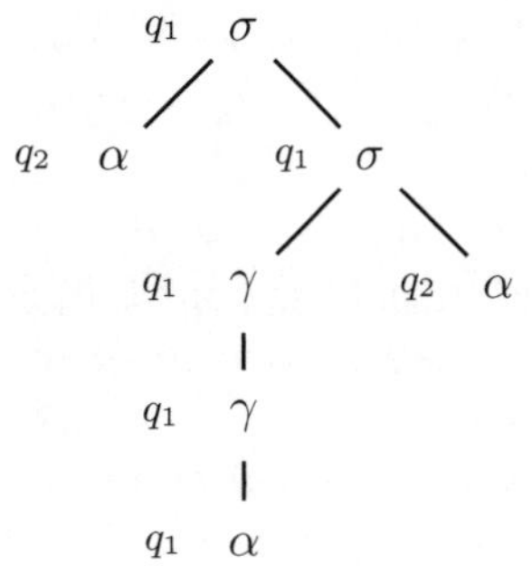

Figure 2: A tree together with a run.

We will denote the pair (ξ, κ) just by κ and indicate ξ by stating $\kappa \in R^q_{\mathcal{A}}(\xi)$. We will also omit the subscript $\mathcal{A}$. We set $R(\xi) = \bigcup_{q \in Q} R^q(\xi)$.

Let $w \in \mathrm{pos}(\xi)$ and $\kappa \in R^q(\xi)$. The following notions are defined in the obvious way: (i) $\kappa|_w \in R^{\kappa(w)}(\xi|_w)$, (ii) $\kappa[\kappa']_w \in R^q(\xi[\xi']_w)$ for every $\xi' \in T_\Sigma(H)$ and $\kappa' \in R^{\kappa(w)}(\xi')$, and (iii) $\kappa \cdot \kappa' \in R^{q'}(\xi \cdot \zeta)$ for every $q' \in Q$, $\zeta \in C_\Sigma$, and $\kappa' \in R^{q'}(\zeta)$ that maps the z-labelled position to q. We will abuse the above notation in two ways: (i) we write $\kappa[z]_w$ to denote $\kappa[\kappa']_w$ where κ' is the only element of $R^{\kappa(w)}(z)$, and (ii) for every $s \in S$, we write $s \cdot \kappa$ to denote the run on $s \cdot \zeta$ which coincides with κ.

Let $\xi \in T_\Sigma(S \cup S^Q)$ and $\kappa \in R(\xi)$. We define the *weight* $\langle\kappa\rangle_{\mathcal{A}} \in S$ *of* κ as follows (omitting the subscript $\mathcal{A}$): if $\xi \in S$, then $\langle\kappa\rangle = \xi$; if $\xi \in S^Q$, then $\langle\kappa\rangle = \xi_{\kappa(\varepsilon)}$; if $\xi = \sigma(\xi_1, \dots, \xi_k)$, then $\langle\kappa\rangle = \langle\kappa|_1\rangle \cdot \dots \cdot \langle\kappa|_k\rangle \cdot \delta(\kappa(1) \cdots \kappa(k), \sigma, \kappa(\varepsilon))$.

We define the mapping $[\![.]\!]_{\mathcal{A}} \colon T_\Sigma(S^Q) \to S^Q$ such that $[\![\xi]\!]_{\mathcal{A}}(q) = \sum_{\kappa \in R^q(\xi)} \langle\kappa\rangle$. Again, we will often omit the subscript $\mathcal{A}$. If we have a factorization (f, g), we will shorten $f([\![\xi]\!])$ to $f[\![\xi]\!]$. We will often use relationships such as $\langle\kappa \cdot \kappa'\rangle = \langle\langle\kappa\rangle \cdot \kappa'\rangle$ and $[\![\xi \cdot \zeta]\!] = [\![[\![\xi]\!] \cdot \zeta]\!]$.

The weighted tree language *run-recognized by* $\mathcal{A}$ is the mapping $\varphi_{\mathcal{A}} \colon T_\Sigma \to S$ such that for every $\xi \in T_\Sigma$ we have $\varphi_{\mathcal{A}}(\xi) = \sum_{q \in Q} [\![\xi]\!]_q \cdot \nu_q$.

Example 2.4 (Ex. 2.3 contd.) Figure 2 shows a tree together with a run κ. We compute $\langle\kappa\rangle$ (recall that we use the arctic semiring):

$$\begin{aligned}
\langle\kappa\rangle &= \langle\kappa|_1\rangle + \langle\kappa|_2\rangle + \delta(q_2 q_1, \sigma, q_1) \\
&= \delta(\varepsilon, \alpha, q_2) + \delta(\varepsilon, \alpha, q_1) + \delta(q_1, \gamma, q_1) \\
&\quad + \delta(q_1, \gamma, q_1) + \delta(\varepsilon, \alpha, q_2) \\
&\quad + \delta(q_1 q_2, \sigma, q_1) + \delta(q_2 q_1, \sigma, q_1) \\
&= 0 + 0 + 1 + 1 + 0 + 1 + 1 = 4 \,.
\end{aligned}$$

It can be shown that $[\![\xi]\!]_{q_1} = \mathrm{ht}(\xi)$ and $[\![\xi]\!]_{q_2} = 0$, and thus, that $\varphi_{\mathcal{A}} = \mathrm{ht}$. □

For every $\xi \in T_\Sigma(S^Q)$ and $\kappa \in R(\xi)$ we call κ *victorious (on ξ)* if $\langle\kappa\rangle = [\![\xi]\!]_{\kappa(\varepsilon)}$. The following observations are based on (Büchse, May and Vogler, 2010, Obs. 5.11 and 5.12).

Observation 2.5 *Let S be an extremal semiring. For every $\xi \in T_\Sigma(S^Q)$ and $q \in Q$ there is a $\kappa \in R^q(\xi)$ such that κ is victorious.*

Observation 2.6 *Let $\xi \in T_\Sigma(S^Q)$, $w \in \mathrm{pos}(\xi)$, and $\kappa \in R(\xi)$ victorious. Then we obtain $\langle\kappa\rangle = [\![(\langle\kappa|_w\rangle \cdot e_{\kappa(w)}) \cdot \xi[z]_w]\!]_{\kappa(\varepsilon)}$.*

PROOF.

$$\begin{aligned}
&[\![(\langle\kappa|_w\rangle \cdot e_{\kappa(w)}) \cdot \xi[z]_w]\!]_{\kappa(\varepsilon)} \\
&= \textstyle\sum_{\kappa' \in R^{\kappa(\varepsilon)}((\langle\kappa|_w\rangle \cdot e_{\kappa(w)}) \cdot \xi[z]_w)} \langle\kappa'\rangle \\
&= \textstyle\sum_{\kappa' \in R^{\kappa(\varepsilon)}(\xi[z]_w), \kappa'(w) = \kappa(w)} \langle\langle\kappa|_w\rangle \cdot \kappa'\rangle \\
&= \textstyle\sum_{\kappa' \in R^{\kappa(\varepsilon)}(\xi[z]_w), \kappa'(w) = \kappa(w)} \langle\kappa|_w \cdot \kappa'\rangle \\
&= \langle\kappa\rangle \,.
\end{aligned}$$

For the last equation, we note that the summands on the left-hand side form a subset of $\{\langle\nu\rangle \mid \nu \in R^{\kappa(\varepsilon)}(\xi)\}$, which contains $\langle\kappa\rangle$. Since S is extremal and $\langle\kappa\rangle = [\![\xi]\!]_{\kappa(\varepsilon)}$, the equation holds. ■

2.5 Twins Property

We define two binary relations $\mathrm{SIBLINGS}(\mathcal{A})$ and $\mathrm{TWINS}(\mathcal{A})$ over Q as follows. Let $p, q \in Q$. Then

- $(p, q) \in \mathrm{SIBLINGS}(\mathcal{A})$ iff there is a tree $\xi \in T_\Sigma$ such that $[\![\xi]\!]_p \neq 0$ and $[\![\xi]\!]_q \neq 0$.
- $(p, q) \in \mathrm{TWINS}(\mathcal{A})$ iff for every context $\zeta \in C_\Sigma$ we have that $[\![e_p \cdot \zeta]\!]_p \neq 0$ and $[\![e_q \cdot \zeta]\!]_q \neq 0$ implies $[\![e_p \cdot \zeta]\!]_p = [\![e_q \cdot \zeta]\!]_q$.

The wta $\mathcal{A}$ is said to have the *twins property* if $\mathrm{SIBLINGS}(\mathcal{A}) \subseteq \mathrm{TWINS}(\mathcal{A})$.

Example 2.7 We cover two examples.

First, consider the wta from Ex. 2.3. Its two states are siblings as witnessed by the tree $\xi = \alpha$. However, they are not twins, as witnessed by the context $\zeta = \gamma(z)$: $[\![e_{q_1} \cdot \gamma(z)]\!]_{q_1} = 1$, whereas $[\![e_{q_2} \cdot \gamma(z)]\!]_{q_2} = 0$.

Second, consider the wta over the Viterbi semiring shown Fig. 3. Its two states are siblings as witnessed by the tree $\xi = \alpha$. Furthermore, they are twins because their transitions are symmetric. Hence, this wta has the twins property. □

The following observation shows that we can enumerate $\mathrm{SIBLINGS}(\mathcal{A})$ in finite time.

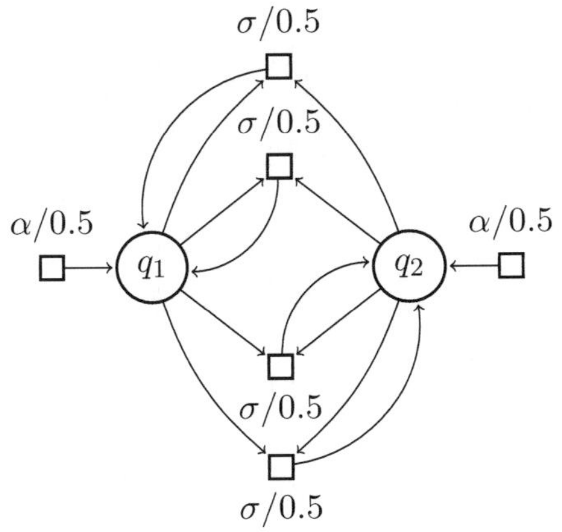

Figure 3: Siblings and twins.

Observation 2.8 *If S is zero-sum free, we have* $\text{SIBLINGS}(\mathcal{A}) = \text{SIB}(\mathcal{A})$ *where* $\text{SIB}(\mathcal{A})$ *is defined like* $\text{SIBLINGS}(\mathcal{A})$*, with the additional condition that* $\text{ht}(\xi) < |Q|^2$.

PROOF. The direction $\supseteq$ is trivial. We show $\subseteq$ by contradiction. Let $p, q \in Q$ and $\xi \in T_\Sigma$ such that (i) $[\![\xi]\!]_p \neq 0$ and $[\![\xi]\!]_q \neq 0$, and (ii) $(p, q) \notin \text{SIB}(\mathcal{A})$. We assume that ξ is smallest, and we show that we find a smaller counterexample.

By (ii), we have (iii) $\text{ht}(\xi) \geq |Q|^2$. By (i), there are $\kappa_p \in R^p(\xi)$ and $\kappa_q \in R^q(\xi)$ such that (iv) $\langle \kappa_p \rangle \neq 0$ and $\langle \kappa_q \rangle \neq 0$.

By (iii), there are positions w_1, w_2 such that w_1 is above w_2, $\kappa_p(w_1) = \kappa_p(w_2)$, and $\kappa_q(w_1) = \kappa_q(w_2)$. Cutting out the slice between w_1 and w_2, we construct the tree $\xi' = \xi[\xi|_{w_2}]_{w_1}$. Moreover, we construct the runs κ'_p and κ'_q accordingly, i.e., $\kappa'_x = \kappa_x[\kappa_x|_{w_2}]_{w_1}$.

We have that $\langle \kappa'_p \rangle \neq 0$, $\langle \kappa'_q \rangle \neq 0$, because otherwise (iv) would be violated. Since S is zero-sum free, we obtain $[\![\xi']\!]_p \neq 0$, $[\![\xi']\!]_q \neq 0$. ∎

3 Decidability of the Twins Property

This section contains our main theorem:

Theorem 3.1 *The twins property of wta over extremal semifields is decidable.*

The following subsections provide the infrastructure and lemmata needed for the proof of the theorem. Henceforth, we assume that S is an extremal semifield. As noted in Ex. 2.2, there is a maximal factorization (f, g).

3.1 Rephrasing the Twins Relation

In the definition of $\text{TWINS}(\mathcal{A})$, we deal with two vectors $[\![e_p \cdot \zeta]\!]$ and $[\![e_q \cdot \zeta]\!]$ for each $\zeta \in C_\Sigma$. In the following we concatenate these vectors into one, which enables us to use a factorization. To this end, we construct a wta $\mathcal{A} \cup \bar{\mathcal{A}}$ that runs two instances of $\mathcal{A}$ in parallel, as shown in Fig. 4.

Let $\mathcal{A} = (Q, \Sigma, S, \delta, \nu)$ a wta and $\bar{\mathcal{A}} = (\bar{Q}, \Sigma, S, \bar{\delta}, \bar{\nu})$ be the wta obtained from $\mathcal{A}$ by renaming states via $q \mapsto \bar{q}$. We construct the wta $\mathcal{A} \cup \bar{\mathcal{A}} = (Q \cup \bar{Q}, \Sigma, S, \delta', \nu')$ where δ' coincides with δ and $\bar{\delta}$ on the transitions of $\mathcal{A}$ and $\bar{\mathcal{A}}$, respectively; it maps all other transitions to 0; and ν' coincides with ν and $\bar{\nu}$ on Q and $\bar{Q}$, respectively.

For every $p, q \in Q$ we define the set $T_{p,q} \subseteq S^{Q \cup \bar{Q}}$ by $T_{p,q} = \{[\![(e_p + e_{\bar{q}}) \cdot \zeta]\!]_{\mathcal{A} \cup \bar{\mathcal{A}}} \mid \zeta \in C_\Sigma\}$; note that $e_p, e_{\bar{q}} \in S^{Q \cup \bar{Q}}$. With this definition, we observe the following trivial equivalence.

Observation 3.2 *Let $p, q \in Q$. Then $(p, q) \in \text{TWINS}(\mathcal{A})$ iff for every $u \in T_{p,q}$ we have that*

$$u_p \neq 0 \text{ and } u_{\bar{q}} \neq 0 \text{ implies } u_p = u_{\bar{q}}.$$

For every pair $(p, q) \in \text{SIBLINGS}(\mathcal{A})$, a vector $u \in S^{Q \cup \bar{Q}}$ is called a *critical vector (for (p, q))* if it does not fulfill the centered implication of Obs. 3.2. Any critical vector in $T_{p,q}$ thereby witnesses $(p, q) \notin \text{TWINS}(\mathcal{A})$. Consequently, $\mathcal{A}$ has the twins property iff $T_{p,q}$ contains no critical vector for any $(p, q) \in \text{SIBLINGS}(\mathcal{A})$. Deciding the twins property thus amounts to searching for a critical vector.

3.2 Compressing the Search Space

In this subsection we approach the decidability of the twins property by compressing the search space for critical vectors. First we show that the vectors in $T_{p,q}$ are scalar multiples of a finite number of vectors.

Lemma 3.3 *Let S be a commutative, extremal semiring. Assume that $\mathcal{A}$ has the twins property. Then there is a finite set $S' \subseteq S^{Q \cup \bar{Q}}$ such that for every $(p, q) \in \text{SIBLINGS}(\mathcal{A})$ we have*

$$T_{p,q} \subseteq S \cdot S'.$$

PROOF. We construct sets $S', S'' \subseteq S^{Q \cup \bar{Q}}$ and show the following inclusions:

$$T_{p,q} \subseteq S \cdot S'' \subseteq S \cdot S'. \qquad (*)$$

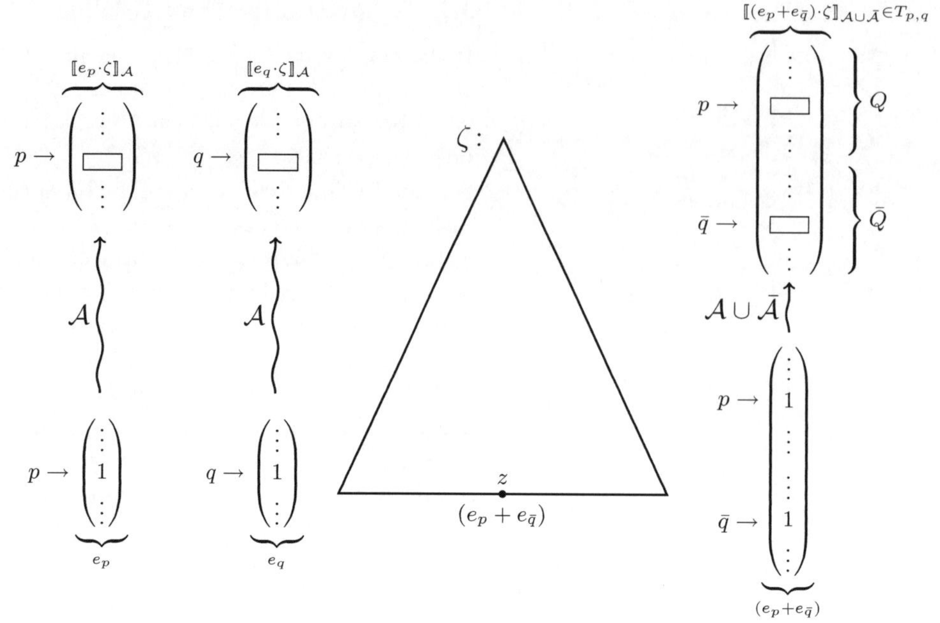

Figure 4: Moving from parallel execution of $\mathcal{A}$ (left-hand side) to the union wta $\mathcal{A} \cup \bar{\mathcal{A}}$ (right-hand side).

To this end, we consider each entry in each vector to be induced by an according (victorious) run. In this spirit we define for every $p, q \in Q$ and $\zeta \in C_\Sigma$ the set $C_{p,q}(\zeta) \subseteq R((e_p + e_{\bar{q}}) \cdot \zeta)^{Q \cup \bar{Q}}$ of vectors of runs of $\mathcal{A} \cup \bar{\mathcal{A}}$ as follows: $\kappa \in C_{p,q}(\zeta)$ iff (i) $\kappa_r \in R^r((e_p + e_{\bar{q}}) \cdot \zeta)$ for every $r \in Q \cup \bar{Q}$ and (ii) for every pair $w_1, w_2 \in \mathrm{pos}(\zeta)$ with w_1 above w_2 and $\kappa_r(w_1) = \kappa_r(w_2)$ we have that $\kappa_r|_{w_1}$ is victorious on $((e_p + e_{\bar{q}}) \cdot \zeta)|_{w_1}$. We map each vector of runs to the corresponding weight vector as follows. For every $Q' \subseteq Q \cup \bar{Q}$ let $\gamma_{Q'} \colon R((e_p + e_{\bar{q}}) \cdot \zeta)^{Q \cup \bar{Q}} \to S^{Q \cup \bar{Q}}$ be the mapping such that for every κ and $q' \in Q \cup \bar{Q}$:

$$\gamma_{Q'}(\kappa)_{q'} = \begin{cases} \langle \kappa_{q'} \rangle & \text{if } q' \in Q' \\ 0 & \text{otherwise.} \end{cases}$$

We set $S'' = \{\gamma_{Q'}(\kappa) \mid (p, q) \in \textsc{Siblings}(\mathcal{A}), \zeta \in C_\Sigma, \kappa \in C_{p,q}(\zeta), Q' \subseteq Q \cup \bar{Q}\}$. The set S' is defined in the same way, with the additional condition that $\mathrm{ht}(\zeta) < 2|Q|^{2|Q|}$.

The first inclusion of $(*)$ can be proved in the same way as (Büchse, May and Vogler, 2010, Lemma 5.14). Here we show the second inclusion by contradiction. To this end, let $s \in S$, $(p, q) \in \textsc{Siblings}(\mathcal{A})$, $\zeta \in C_\Sigma$, $\kappa \in C_{p,q}(\zeta)$, and $Q' \subseteq Q \cup \bar{Q}$ such that $s \cdot \gamma_{Q'}(\kappa) \notin S \cdot S'$, and thus $\mathrm{ht}(\zeta) \geq 2|Q|^{2|Q|}$. We can assume that $\langle \kappa_r \rangle \neq 0$ for every $r \in Q'$ because otherwise we could adjust Q' without harm. Finally, we assume that ζ is smallest.

We will construct a new context ζ' and a corresponding vector $\kappa' \in C_{p,q}(\zeta')$ such that ζ' is smaller than ζ and $s \cdot \gamma_{Q'}(\kappa) = s \cdot s' \cdot \gamma_{Q'}(\kappa')$ for some $s' \in S$. Then, if the right-hand side is in $S \cdot S'$, so is the left-hand side. By contraposition, this shows that ζ was not a smallest counterexample, yielding the contradiction.

First, let w be the position in ζ labelled z. We show that we are able to find a pair (w_1, w_2) of positions such that w_1 is above w_2, $\kappa_r(w_1) = \kappa_r(w_2)$ for every r, and either both or none of w_1 and w_2 are above w. To this end, we distinguish two cases (cf. Fig. 5).

(a) If $|w| \leq |Q|^{2|Q|}$, then the length of the common prefix of w and any path of length at least $2|Q|^{2|Q|}$ can be at most $|Q|^{2|Q|}$. Hence, on such a path remain at least $|Q|^{2|Q|} + 1$ positions that are not above w. By the pidgeonhole principle, we find said pair (w_1, w_2).

(b) If $|w| > |Q|^{2|Q|}$, then we find the pair immediately on the path to the position labelled z.

Second, we pick a pair (w_1, w_2) such that the position w_1 has minimal length. Cutting out the slice between the positions w_1 and w_2 yields the smaller context $\zeta' = \zeta[\zeta|_{w_2}]_{w_1}$. We construct κ' accordingly, i.e., $\kappa'_r = \kappa_r[\kappa_r|_{w_2}]_{w_1}$ for every $r \in Q \cup \bar{Q}$. We have that $\kappa' \in C_{p,q}(\zeta')$; for this we

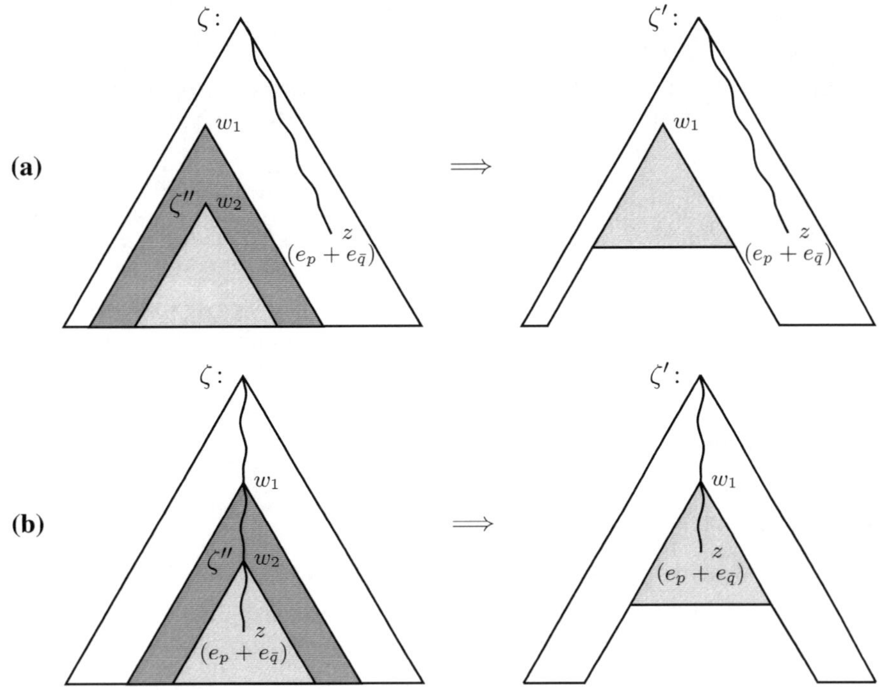

Figure 5: Two cases for the construction of $\zeta' = \zeta[\zeta|_{w_2}]_{w_1}$.

need that we chose w_1 with minimal length.

Third, we use the twins property to show that there is an $s' \in S$ such that $s \cdot \gamma_{Q'}(\kappa) = s \cdot s' \cdot \gamma_{Q'}(\kappa')$. If $Q' = \emptyset$, we set $s' = 0$, and the proof is done. Otherwise we choose some $r' \in Q'$ and set $s' = [\![e_{\kappa_{r'}(w_2)} \cdot \zeta'']\!]_{\kappa_{r'}(w_1)}$ where $\zeta'' = \zeta[z]_{w_2}|_{w_1}$ is the slice we have cut out. We prove that $\gamma_{Q'}(\kappa) = s' \cdot \gamma_{Q'}(\kappa')$. To this end, let $r \in Q'$, $p' = \kappa_r(w_1) = \kappa_r(w_2)$, and $q' = \kappa_{r'}(w_1) = \kappa_{r'}(w_2)$. Then

$$
\begin{aligned}
\gamma_{Q'}(\kappa)_r &= \langle \kappa_r \rangle = \langle \langle \kappa_r|_{w_1} \rangle \cdot \kappa_r[z]_{w_1} \rangle \\
&= \langle [\![(\langle \kappa_r|_{w_2} \rangle \cdot e_{p'}) \cdot \zeta'']\!]_{p'} \cdot \kappa_r[z]_{w_1} \rangle \quad \text{(Obs. 2.6)} \\
&= \langle \kappa_r|_{w_2} \rangle \cdot [\![e_{p'} \cdot \zeta'']\!]_{p'} \cdot \langle 1 \cdot \kappa_r[z]_{w_1} \rangle \\
&\qquad \text{(commutativity)} \\
&= \langle \kappa_r|_{w_2} \rangle \cdot [\![e_{q'} \cdot \zeta'']\!]_{q'} \cdot \langle 1 \cdot \kappa_r[z]_{w_1} \rangle \quad (\dagger) \\
&= s' \cdot \langle \langle \kappa_r|_{w_2} \rangle \cdot \kappa_r[z]_{w_1} \rangle \quad \text{(commutativity)} \\
&= s' \cdot \langle \kappa'_r \rangle = s' \cdot \gamma_{Q'}(\kappa')_r \,.
\end{aligned}
$$

At (†) we have used the twins property. We show that this is justified. First, we show that $(p', q') \in$ SIBLINGS$(\mathcal{A} \cup \bar{\mathcal{A}})$. To this end, we distinguish two cases.

If z occurs in $\zeta|_{w_2}$: by $(p, q) \in$ SIBLINGS$(\mathcal{A})$ we obtain a tree ξ such that $[\![\xi]\!]_p \neq 0$ and $[\![\xi]\!]_q \neq 0$. By our assumption we have $\langle \kappa_r \rangle \neq 0$, $\langle \kappa_{r'} \rangle \neq 0$, and thus, $\langle \kappa_r|_{w_2} \rangle \neq 0$, $\langle \kappa_{r'}|_{w_2} \rangle \neq 0$. Since S is extremal, and thus, zero-sum free, we obtain $[\![\xi \cdot \zeta|_{w_2}]\!]_{p'} \neq 0$, $[\![\xi \cdot \zeta|_{w_2}]\!]_{q'} \neq 0$.

If z does not occur in $\zeta|_{w_2}$: we derive in a similar fashion that $\langle \kappa_r|_{w_2} \rangle \neq 0$, $\langle \kappa_{r'}|_{w_2} \rangle \neq 0$, and thus, $[\![\zeta|_{w_2}]\!]_{p'} \neq 0$, $[\![\zeta|_{w_2}]\!]_{q'} \neq 0$.

Second, by the twins property, we have that $(p', q') \in$ TWINS$(\mathcal{A} \cup \bar{\mathcal{A}})$. Using again that $\langle \kappa_r \rangle \neq 0$, $\langle \kappa_{r'} \rangle \neq 0$, we derive $\langle \kappa_r[z]_{w_2}|_{w_1} \rangle \neq 0$, $\langle \kappa_{r'}[z]_{w_2}|_{w_1} \rangle \neq 0$. Hence, $[\![e_{p'} \cdot \zeta'']\!]_{p'} \neq 0$, $[\![e_{q'} \cdot \zeta'']\!]_{q'} \neq 0$. Consequently, we have (†). ■

We note that $u \in S^{Q \cup \bar{Q}}$, $u \neq \tilde{0}$, is a critical vector iff $f(u)$ is a critical vector. Hence, applying the factorization to $T_{p,q}$ for every $(p, q) \in$ SIBLINGS$(\mathcal{A})$ results in a compressed search space for critical vectors. It follows from the preceding lemma that the resulting search space is finite.

Lemma 3.4 *Let (f, g) be a maximal factorization of dimension $Q \cup \bar{Q}$. Assume that $\mathcal{A}$ has the twins property. For every $(p, q) \in$ SIBLINGS$(\mathcal{A})$ the set $f(T_{p,q} \setminus \{\tilde{0}\})$ is finite.*

PROOF. By Lemma 3.3 there is a finite set S' with

$$f(T_{p,q} \setminus \{\tilde{0}\}) \subseteq f(S \cdot S') \subseteq f(S') \,,$$

where we used that (f, g) is maximal. Since S' is finite, so is $f(T_{p,q} \setminus \{\tilde{0}\})$. ■

Algorithm 1 Decision algorithm

Require: $\mathcal{A} = (Q, \Sigma, S, \delta, \nu)$ a wta, S commutative, extremal, (f, g) maximal factorization

Ensure: print "yes" iff $\mathcal{A}$ has the twins property

1: compute SIBLINGS($\mathcal{A}$)
2: **for** $(p, q) \in$ SIBLINGS($\mathcal{A}$) in parallel **do**
3:     **for** $u \in f(T_{p,q} \setminus \{\tilde{0}\})$ **do**
4:         **if** u is a critical vector **then**
5:             print "no" and terminate
6: print "yes"

3.3 Two Decision Algorithms

In this section we consider two decision algorithms. The first one is part of the following proof.

PROOF (OF THM. 3.1). Algorithm 1 proceeds as follows. First, it enumerates SIBLINGS($\mathcal{A}$). This is possible as shown by Obs. 2.8. Second, for each $(p, q) \in$ SIBLINGS($\mathcal{A}$) in parallel, it enumerates $f(T_{p,q} \setminus \{\tilde{0}\})$, checking for critical vectors. For this step, we distinguish two cases.

Either $\mathcal{A}$ has the twins property. Then, by Lemma 3.4, $f(T_{p,q} \setminus \{\tilde{0}\})$ is finite, and the algorithm will terminate without finding any critical vector, in which case it outputs "yes".

Or $\mathcal{A}$ does not have the twins property, but then, by Obs. 3.2, the algorithm is guaranteed to find a critical vector at some point, in which case it outputs "no". Note that the parallel processing (line 2) is critical in this case because there may be $(p, q) \in$ SIBLINGS($\mathcal{A}$) such that $f(T_{p,q} \setminus \{\tilde{0}\})$ is infinite, but does not contain a critical vector. ■

Note that Algorithm 1 basically enumerates the set $\bigcup_{(p,q) \in \text{SIBLINGS}(\mathcal{A})} f(T_{p,q} \setminus \{\tilde{0}\})$. In principle, this can be done by enumerating C_Σ and computing $f[\![(e_p + e_{\bar{q}}) \cdot \zeta]\!]$ for each $\zeta \in C_\Sigma$. However, the computation of weights already done for subcontexts of ζ is not reused in this approach.

In the following we show an alternative procedure (Algorithm 2) that does not enumerate C_Σ explicitly but works on weight vectors instead, thereby avoiding redundant calculation. This procedure maintains a pair of subsets of $S^{Q \cup \bar{Q}}$. It begins with $(\emptyset, \emptyset)$ and keeps adding vectors by applying a monotone operation F until either the second component contains a critical vector or no new vectors are added.

To this end, we define the unary operation F over pairs of subsets of $S^{Q \cup \bar{Q}}$ by $(T, C) \mapsto$

Algorithm 2 Improved decision algorithm

Require: $\mathcal{A} = (Q, \Sigma, S, \delta, \nu)$ a wta, S commutative, extremal, (f, g) maximal factorization

Ensure: print "yes" iff $\mathcal{A}$ has the twins property

compute SIBLINGS($\mathcal{A}$)
$(T, C) \leftarrow (\emptyset, \emptyset)$
repeat
    $(T', C') \leftarrow (T, C)$
    $(T, C) \leftarrow F(T', C')$ ▷ uses SIBLINGS($\mathcal{A}$)
until C contains critical vector or $C = C'$
if critical vector has been found **then**
    print "no"
else
    print "yes"

(T', C') where T' and C' contain exactly the following elements:

(F1) for every $k \geq 0$, $\sigma \in \Sigma^{(k)}$, and $u_1, \ldots, u_k \in T$, if $[\![\sigma(u_1, \ldots, u_k)]\!] \neq \tilde{0}$, then $f[\![\sigma(u_1, \ldots, u_k)]\!] \in T'$,

(F2) for every $(p, q) \in$ SIBLINGS($\mathcal{A}$), we have $f(e_p + e_{\bar{q}}) \in C'$,

(F3) for every $k \geq 1$, $\sigma \in \Sigma^{(k)}$, $i \in \{1, \ldots, k\}$, $u_i \in C$, and $u_1, \ldots, u_{i-1}, u_{i+1}, \ldots, u_k \in T$, if $[\![\sigma(u_1, \ldots, u_k)]\!] \neq \tilde{0}$, then $f[\![\sigma(u_1, \ldots, u_k)]\!] \in C'$.

Kleene's fixpoint theorem (Wechler, 1992, Sec. 1.5.2, Theorem 7) yields that F has a least fixpoint (where we use the pointwise subset order), and that it can be calculated by the saturation procedure outlined above. In the forthcoming Lemma 3.6, we show that said fixpoint contains the desired set $\bigcup_{(p,q) \in \text{SIBLINGS}(\mathcal{A})} f(T_{p,q} \setminus \{\tilde{0}\})$. This implies both the correctness of our procedure and its termination, by the same line of reasoning as for Algorithm 1. As a preparation we recall two auxiliary statements.

Observation 3.5 *Let S be commutative and (f, g) maximal. Then for every $k \geq 0$, $\sigma \in \Sigma^{(k)}$, and $\xi_1, \ldots, \xi_k \in T_\Sigma(S^Q)$, we have that* $[\![\sigma(\xi_1, \ldots, \xi_k)]\!] = [\![\sigma([\![\xi_1]\!], \ldots, [\![\xi_k]\!])]\!]$ *and* $f[\![\sigma([\![\xi_1]\!], \ldots, [\![\xi_k]\!])]\!] = f[\![\sigma(f[\![\xi_1]\!], \ldots, f[\![\xi_k]\!])]\!]$.

PROOF. By (Fülöp and Vogler, 2009, Sec 3.2) and (Büchse, May and Vogler, 2010, Lemma 5.5), respectively. ■

Lemma 3.6 *Let (T^f, C^f) be the least fixpoint of F. Then (i) $T^f = f([\![T_\Sigma]\!] \setminus \{\tilde{0}\})$ and (ii) $C^f = \bigcup_{(p,q) \in \text{SIBLINGS}(\mathcal{A})} f(T_{p,q} \setminus \{\tilde{0}\})$.*

PROOF. In this proof we will often use Obs. 3.5.

For "$\subseteq$" of Statement (i), we refer to (Büchse, May and Vogler, 2010, Lemma 5.8).

We prove "$\supseteq$" of Statement (i) by contradiction. To this end, let $\xi \in T_\Sigma$ a smallest tree such that $[\![\xi]\!] \neq \tilde{0}$ and $f[\![\xi]\!] \notin T^f$. By definition of T_Σ, there are $k \geq 0$, $\sigma \in \Sigma^{(k)}$, and $\xi_1, \ldots, \xi_k \in T_\Sigma$ such that $\xi = \sigma(\xi_1, \ldots, \xi_k)$. We derive

$$\begin{aligned} f[\![\sigma(\xi_1, \ldots, \xi_k)]\!] &= f[\![\sigma([\![\xi_1]\!], \ldots, [\![\xi_k]\!])]\!] \\ &= f[\![\sigma(f[\![\xi_1]\!], \ldots, f[\![\xi_k]\!])]\!] \,. \end{aligned}$$

Now either $f[\![\xi_i]\!] \in T^f$ for every $i \in \{1, \ldots, k\}$, but then so is $f[\![\xi]\!]$, or ξ was not the smallest counterexample.

For "$\subseteq$" of Statement (ii), we show that $\left(T^f, \bigcup_{(p,q) \in \mathrm{SIBLINGS}(\mathcal{A})} f(T_{p,q} \setminus \{\tilde{0}\})\right)$ is a prefixpoint of F. It is easy to see that (F1) and (F2) hold. Now let $k, \sigma, i, u_1, \ldots, u_k$ as in (F3) such that $[\![\sigma(u_1, \ldots, u_k)]\!] \neq \tilde{0}$. Hence, $u_1, \ldots, u_k \neq \tilde{0}$. By (i) there are $\xi_1, \ldots, \xi_{i-1}, \xi_{i+1}, \ldots, \xi_k$ such that $u_j = f[\![\xi_j]\!]$ for $j \neq i$. Moreover there are $(p,q) \in \mathrm{SIBLINGS}(\mathcal{A})$ and $\zeta_i \in C_\Sigma$ such that $u_i = f[\![(e_p + e_{\bar{q}}) \cdot \zeta_i]\!]$. We derive

$$\begin{aligned} &f[\![\sigma(u_1, \ldots, u_k)]\!] \\ &= f[\![\sigma(f[\![\xi_1]\!], \ldots, f[\![(e_p + e_{\bar{q}}) \cdot \zeta_i]\!], \ldots, f[\![\xi_k]\!])]\!] \\ &= f[\![\sigma([\![\xi_1]\!], \ldots, [\![(e_p + e_{\bar{q}}) \cdot \zeta_i]\!], \ldots, [\![\xi_k]\!])]\!] \\ &= f[\![\sigma(\xi_1, \ldots, (e_p + e_{\bar{q}}) \cdot \zeta_i, \ldots, \xi_k)]\!] \\ &= f[\![(e_p + e_{\bar{q}}) \cdot \sigma(\xi_1, \ldots, \zeta_i, \ldots, \xi_k)]\!] \,, \end{aligned}$$

which, by definition, is in $f(T_{p,q} \setminus \{\tilde{0}\})$.

We prove "$\supseteq$" of (ii) by contradiction. To this end, let $(p,q) \in \mathrm{SIBLINGS}(\mathcal{A})$ and $\zeta \in C_\Sigma$ a smallest context such that $f[\![(e_p + e_{\bar{q}}) \cdot \zeta]\!] \in f(T_{p,q} \setminus \{\tilde{0}\}) \setminus C^f$. Hence, $[\![(e_p + e_{\bar{q}}) \cdot \zeta]\!] \neq \tilde{0}$. By (F2), we obtain $\zeta \neq z$. Hence, there are $k \geq 1$, $\sigma \in \Sigma^{(k)}$, $i \in \{1, \ldots, k\}$, $\xi_1, \ldots, \xi_{i-1}, \xi_{i+1}, \ldots, \xi_k \in T_\Sigma$, and $\zeta_i \in C_\Sigma$ such that $\zeta = \sigma(\xi_1, \ldots, \xi_{i-1}, \zeta_i, \xi_{i+1}, \ldots, \xi_k)$. We have that $[\![\xi_j]\!] \neq \tilde{0}$ for $j \neq i$, and $[\![(e_p + e_{\bar{q}}) \cdot \zeta_i]\!] \neq \tilde{0}$. We derive

$$\begin{aligned} &f[\![(e_p + e_{\bar{q}}) \cdot \zeta]\!] \\ &= f[\![(e_p + e_{\bar{q}}) \cdot \sigma(\xi_1, \ldots, \zeta_i, \ldots, \xi_k)]\!] \\ &= f[\![\sigma(\xi_1, \ldots, (e_p + e_{\bar{q}}) \cdot \zeta_i, \ldots, \xi_k)]\!] \\ &= f[\![\sigma([\![\xi_1]\!], \ldots, [\![(e_p + e_{\bar{q}}) \cdot \zeta_i]\!], \ldots, [\![\xi_k]\!])]\!] \\ &= f[\![\sigma(f[\![\xi_1]\!], \ldots, f[\![(e_p + e_{\bar{q}}) \cdot \zeta_i]\!], \ldots, f[\![\xi_k]\!])]\!] \end{aligned}$$

By (i), we have that $f[\![\xi_j]\!] \in T^f$. Now either $f[\![(e_p + e_{\bar{q}}) \cdot \zeta_i]\!] \in C^f$, but then so is $f[\![(e_p + e_{\bar{q}}) \cdot \zeta]\!]$, or ζ was not the smallest counterexample. ■

4 Discussion and Further Research

The notion that the twins property can be decided by searching for critical vectors in a compressed search space is due to Kirsten (2012). We have generalized his work in two ways: (i) We allow arbitrary extremal semifields instead of the tropical semiring. To this end, we use the notion of a maximal factorization, which is implicit in his work. (ii) We consider weighted tree automata instead of weighted string automata. This makes the proof more complex, as we have to distinguish between contexts and trees.

Kirsten's result that deciding the twins property is PSPACE-hard directly transfers to our setting, giving a lower bound on the complexity of our algorithms. In addition, he shows that the problem is PSPACE-complete by giving an algorithm that is in PSPACE. We did not investigate whether this result can be transferred to our setting as well.

To check for critical vectors, Algorithm 1 does not need all components from the vectors in $T_{p,q}$ but only the p- and $\bar{q}$-components; thus in the proof of Lemma 3.3 the height restriction $\mathrm{ht}(\zeta) \leq 2|Q|^{2|Q|}$ for S' can ultimately be lowered to $\mathrm{ht}(\zeta) \leq 2|Q|^2$. It is an open question which of the two algorithms performs better in practice.

For further research, it would be interesting to investigate sufficient properties for determinizability that do not require the semifield to be extremal. Then the determinized wta could truly aggregate the weights of the original runs.

Acknowledgments

The authors wish to thank Heiko Vogler for stimulating remarks on a draft, as well as the anonymous referees for pointing out mistakes. The first author was financially supported by DFG VO 1011/6-1.

References

Büchse, Matthias and May, Jonathan and Vogler, Heiko. 2010. Determinization of Weighted Tree Automata using Factorizations. *J. Autom. Lang. Comb.*, 15(3/4).

Casacuberta, Francisco and de la Higuera, Colin. 2000. Computational complexity of problems on probabilistic grammars and transducers. In *Proc. ICGI*, LNCS. Springer.

Chiang, David. 2007. Hierarchical phrase-based translation. *Comp. Ling.*, 33(2):201–228.

Droste, Manfred and Kuich, Werner and Vogler, Heiko, editors. 2009. *Handbook of Weighted Automata*. EATCS Monographs in Theoretical Computer Science. Springer.

Eppstein, David. 1998. Finding the k shortest paths. *SIAM Journal on Computing*, 28(2):652–673.

Ésik, Zoltán and Kuich, Werner. 2003. Formal tree series. *J. Autom. Lang. Comb.*, 8(2):219–285.

Fülöp, Zoltán and Vogler, Heiko. 2009. Weighted tree automata and tree transducers. In (Droste, Kuich and Vogler, 2009), Chapter 9.

Goguen, Joseph. A. and Thatcher, James W. and Wagner, Eric G. and Wright, Jesse B. 1977. Initial Algebra Semantics and Continuous Algebras. *J. ACM*, 24(1):68–95.

Golan, Jonathan Samuel. 1999. *Semirings and their Applications*. Kluwer Academic Publishers.

Graehl, Jonathan and Knight, Kevin and May, Jonathan. 2008. Training tree transducers. *Comp. Ling.*, 34(3):391–427.

Hebisch, Udo and Weinert, Hanns Joachim. 1998. *Semirings: Algebraic Theory and Applications in Computer Science*, Series in Algebra, volume 5. World Scientific.

Huang, Liang and Chiang, David. 2005. Better k-best parsing. In *Proc. IWPT*, pp. 53–64. ACL.

Kirsten, Daniel. 2012. Decidability, Undecidability, and PSPACE-Completeness of the Twins Property in the Tropical Semiring. *Theoretical Computer Science*, 420:56–63.

Kirsten, Daniel and Mäurer, Ina. 2005. On the determinization of weighted automata. *J. Autom. Lang. Comb.*, 10:287–312.

Li, Zhifei and Eisner, Jason and Khudanpur, Sanjeev. 2009. Variational decoding for statistical machine translation. In *Proc. ACL-IJCNLP*, pp. 593–601. ACL.

Mahr, Bernd. 1984. Iteration and summability in semirings. *Annals of Discrete Mathematics*, 19:229–256.

May, Jonathan and Knight, Kevin. 2006. A better N-best list: practical determinization of weighted finite tree automata. In *Proc. NAACL-HLT*, pp. 351–358. ACL.

Pauls, Adam and Klein, Dan. 2009. k-best A* parsing. In *Proc. ACL-IJCNLP*, pp. 958–966. ACL.

Petrov, Slav and Barrett, Leon and Thibaux, Romain and Klein, Dan. 2006. Learning accurate, compact, and interpretable tree annotation. In *Proc. COLING-ACL*, pp. 433-440.

Sima'an, Khalil. 1996. Computational complexity of probabilistic disambiguation by means of tree-grammars. In *Proc. COLING*, pp. 1175–1180. ACL.

Wechler, Wolfgang. 1992. *Universal Algebra for Computer Scientists*, volume 25 of *Monogr. Theoret. Comput. Sci. EATCS Ser.* Springer.

Zhang, Min and Jiang, Hongfei and Aw, Aiti and Li, Haizhou and Tanm, Chew Lim and Li, Sheng 2008. A tree sequence alignment-based tree-to-tree translation model. In *Proc. ACL*, pp. 559–567. ACL.

TTT: A tree transduction language for syntactic and semantic processing

Adam Purtee
University of Rochester
Department of Computer Science
apurtee@cs.rochester.edu

Lenhart Schubert
University of Rochester
Department of Computer Science
schubert@cs.rochester.edu

Abstract

In this paper we present the tree to tree transduction language, TTT. We motivate the overall "template-to-template" approach to the design of the language, and outline its constructs, also providing some examples. We then show that TTT allows transparent formalization of rules for parse tree refinement and correction, logical form refinement and predicate disambiguation, inference, and verbalization of logical forms.

1 Introduction

Pattern matching and pattern-driven transformations of list-structured symbolic expressions or trees are fundamental tools in AI. They facilitate many symbol manipulation tasks, including operations on parse trees and logical forms, and even inference and aspects of dialogue and translation.

The TTT system allows concise and transparent specification of rules for such tasks, in particular (as we will show), parse tree refinement and correction, predicate disambiguation, logical form refinement, inference, and verbalization into English.

In parse tree refinement, our particular focus has been on repair of malformed parses of image captions, as obtained by the Charniak-Johnson parser (Charniak and Johnson, 2005). This has encompassed such tasks as distinguishing passive participles from past participles and temporal nominals from non-temporal ones, among other tasks which will be discussed later. For example, standard treebank parses tag both past participles (as in "has written") and passive participles (as in "was written") as VBN. This is undesirable for subsequent compositional interpretation, as the meanings of past and passive participles are distinct. We can easily relabel the past participles as VBEN by looking for parse tree subexpressions where a VBN is preceded by a form of "have", either immediately or with an intervening adverb or adverbial, and replacing VBN by VBEN in such subexpressions. Of course this can be accomplished in a standard symbol manipulation language like Lisp, but the requisite multiple lines of code obscure the simple nature of the task. We have also been able to repair systematic PP (prepositional phrase) misattachments, at least in the limited domain of image captions. For example, a common error is attachment of a PP to the last conjunct of a conjunction, where instead the entire conjunction should be modified by the PP. Thus when a statistically obtained parse of the sentence " Tanya and Grandma Lillian at her highschool graduation party" brackets as "Tanya and (Grandma Lillian (at her highschool graduation party.))", we want to lift the PP so that "at her highschool graduation party" modifies "Tanya and Grandma Lillian".

Another systematic error is faulty classification of relative pronouns/determiners as wh-question pronouns/determiners, e.g., "the student *whose* mother contacted you" vs. "I know *whose* mother contacted you" – an important distinction in compositional semantics. (Note that only the first occurrence, i.e., the relative determiner, can be paraphrased as *with the property that his*, and only the second occurrence, in which *whose* forms a wh-nominal, can be paraphrased as *the person with the property that his.*) An important point here is that detecting the relative-determiner status of a wh-word like *whose* may require taking account of an arbitrarily deep context. For example, in the phrase "the student in front of whose parents you are standing", *whose* lies two levels of phrasal structure below the nominal it is semantically bound to. Such phenomena motivate the devices in TTT for detecting "vertical patterns" of arbitrary depth. Furthermore, we need to be able to make local changes "on the fly" in matching vertical patterns, because the full set of tree fragments flanking a vertical match cannot in general be saved using match variables. In the case of a wh-word that is to be re-tagged as a relative word, we need to rewrite it *at the point where the vertical pattern matches it*, rather than in a separate tree-(re)construction phase following the tree-matching phase.

An example of a discourse phenomenon that requires vertical matching is anaphoric referent determination. In particular, consider the well-known rule that a viable referent for an anaphoric pronoun is an NP that C-commands it, i.e., that is a (usually left) sibling of an ancestor of the pronoun. For example, in the sentence "John shows Lillian the snowman that he built", the NP for *John* C-commands the pronominal NP for *he*, and thus is a viable referent for it (modulo gender and number agreement). We will later show a simple TTT rule that tags such an anaphoric pronoun with the indices of its C-commanding NP nodes, thus setting the stage for semantic interpretation.

We have also been able to perform Skolemization, conjunct separation, simple inference, and logical form verbalization with TTT and suspect its utility to logic tasks will increase as development continues.

The rest of the paper is organized as follows: we discuss related work in section 2, discuss the TTT language (including pattern matching and transduction syntax, and some theoretical properties) in section 3, and go though several detailed example applications in section 4.

A beta version of the system can be found at *http://www.cs.rochester.edu/research/ttt/*.

2 Related Work

There are several pattern matching and transduction facilities available; however, none proved sufficiently general and perspicuous to serve our various purposes. The Tiburon tool is a comprehensive system for manipulating regular tree grammars, tree automata, and tree transducers, including weighted variants (May and Knight, 2008). It supports many useful algorithms, such as intersection, determinization, recognition, top-k generation, and maximum likelihood training. However, variables that appear in both a rule's lhs and rhs must occur at a depth less than two on the left, and Tiburon cannot easily simulate our vertical path or sequence operators.

Timbuk is a system for deciding reachability with term rewriting systems and tree automata (Genet, 2003), and it also performs intersection, union, and determinization of tree automata. Though variables can appear at arbitrary locations in terms, they always match exactly one term from a fixed set, and therefore do not match sequences or vertical paths.

The three related tools Tgrep, Tregex, and Tsurgeon provide powerful tree matching and restructuring capabilities (Levy and Andrew, 2006). However, Tgrep and Tregex provide no transduction mechanism, and Tsurgeon's modifications are limited to local transformations on trees. Also, it presupposes list structures that begin with an atom (as in Treebank trees, but not in parse trees with explicit phrasal features), and its patterns are fundamentally tree traversal patterns rather than tree templates, and can be quite hard to read.

Xpath and XSLT are languages for manipulation of XML trees (World Wide Web Consortium, 1999; World Wide Web Consortium, 1999). As its name indicates, Xpath expressions describe paths in trees to the relevant nodes, rather than patterns representing the trees to be matched, as in the TTT approach. It is useful for extracting structured but unordered information from trees, and supports numerous functions and predicates over matched nodes, but does not match ordered sequences. XSLT is also more procedurally oriented than TTT, and is useful for constructing XML representations of transformations of data extracted by Xpath. The primary advantages of TTT over Xpath and XSLT are a more concise syntax, ordered sequence matching, compositional patterns and templates, and in-place modification of trees.

Peter Norvig's pattern matching language, "pat-match", from (Norvig, 1991) provides a nice pattern matching facility within the Lisp environment, allowing for explicit templates with variables (that can bind subexpressions or sequences of them), and including ways to apply arbitrary tests to expressions and to match boolean combinations of patterns. However, there is no provision for "vertical" pattern matching or subexpression replacement "on the fly", which are features of TTT we have found useful. Also the notation for alternatives, along with exclusions, is more concise than in Norvig's matcher, for instance not requiring explicit ORs. Like TTT, pat-match supports matching multi-level structures, but unlike TTT, the pattern operators are not composable.

Mathematica also allows for sophisticated pattern matching, including matching of sequences and trees. It also includes a term rewriting system that is also capable of rewriting ordered sequences. It provides functions to apply patterns to arbitrary subtrees of a tree until all matches have been found or some threshold count is reached, and it can return all possible ways of applying a set of rules to an expression. However, as in the case of Norvig's matcher there is no provision for vertical patterns or on-the-fly transduction (Wolfram Research, Inc, 2010).

3 TTT

Pattern Matching

Patterns in TTT are hierarchically composed of sub-patterns. The simplest kind of pattern is an arbitrary, explicit list structure (tree) containing no match operators, and this will match only an identical list structure. Slightly more flexible patterns are enabled by the "underscore operators" `_!`, `_+`, `_?`, `_*`. These match any single tree, any non-empty sequence of trees, the empty sequence or a sequence of one tree, and any (empty or non-empty) sequence of trees respectively. These operators (as well as all others) can also be thought of as match variables, as they pick up the tree or sequence of trees they match as their binding.

The bindings are "non-sticky", i.e., an operator such as `_!` will match any tree, causing replacement of any prior binding (within the same pattern) by that tree. However, bindings can be preserved in two ways: by use of new variable names, or by use of sticky variables. New variable names are obtained by appending additional characters – conventionally, digits – to the basic ones, e.g., `_!1`, `_!2`, etc. Sticky variables are written with a dot, i.e., `_!.`, `_+.`, `_?.`, `_*.`, where again these symbols may be followed by additional digits or other characters. The important point concerning sticky variables is that multiple occurrences of such a variable in a pattern can only be bound by the same unique value. Transductions are specified by a special pattern operator / and will be described in the next section.

More flexible operators, allowing for alternatives, negation, and vertical patterns among other constructs, are written as a list headed by an operator without an underscore, followed by one or more arguments. For example, `(! A (B C))` will match either the symbol `A` or the list `(B C)`, i.e., the two arguments provide alternatives. As an example involving negation, `(+ A (B _!) ~ (B B))` will match any nonempty sequence whose elements are `A`s or two-element lists headed by `B`, but disallowing elements of type `(B B)`. Successful matches cause the matched expression or sequence of expressions to become the value of the operator. Again, sticky versions of match operators use a dot, and the operators may be extended by appending digits or other characters.

The ten basic argument-taking pattern operators are:

- ! Match exactly one sub-pattern argument.
- + Match a sequence of one or more arguments.
- ? Match the empty sequence or one argument.
- * Match the empty sequence or one or more arguments.
- {} Match any permutation of the arguments.
- <> Match the sequence of arguments directly (without the parenthesis enclosing the <> operator)
- ^ Match a tree that has a child matching one of the arguments.
- ^* Match a tree that has a descendant matching one of the arguments.
- ^@ Match a vertical path.
- / Attempt a transduction. (Explained later.)

Various examples will be provided below. Any of the arguments to a pattern operator may be composed of arbitrary patterns.

Negation: The operators `!`, `+`, `?`, `*`, and `^` support negation (pattern exclusion); i.e., the arguments of these operators may include not only alternatives, but also a negation sign ~ (after the alternatives) that is immediately followed by one or more precluded patterns. If no alternatives are provided, only precluded patterns, this is interpreted as "anything goes", except for the precluded patterns. For example, `(+ ~ (A A) B)` will match any nonempty sequence of expressions that contains no elements of type `(A A)` or `B`. Note that the negation operator does not appear by itself; one must instead specify it in conjunction with one of the other operators. The pattern `(! ~ P)` matches any single tree which does not match pattern `P`.

Conjunction: We have so far found no compelling need for an explicit conjunction operator. If necessary, a way to say that a tree must match each of two or more patterns is to use double negation. For example, suppose we want to say that an expression must begin with an `A` or `B` but must contain an `A` (at the top level); this could be expressed as
`(! ~ (! ~ ((! A B) _*) (_* A _*)))`.
However, this would be more perspicuously expressed in terms of alternatives, i.e.,
`(! (A _*) (B _* A _*))`.
We also note that the allowance for computable predicates (discussed below) enables introduction of a simple construct like
`(! (and? P1 P2))`, where `P1` and `P2` are arbitrary TTT patterns, and `and?` is an executable predicate that applies the TTT matcher to its arguments and returns a non-nil value if both succeed and nil otherwise. In the former case, the binding of the outer `!` will become the matched tree.

Bounded Iteration: The operators `!`, `+`, `?`, `*`, and `^` also support bounded iteration, using square brackets. This enables one to write patterns that match exactly `n`, at least `n`, at most `n`, or from `n` to `m` times, where `n` and `m` are integers. Eg. `(![3] A)` would match the sequence `A A A`. The vertical operator `^[n]` matches trees with a depth-`n` descendant that matches one of the operator's arguments.

Vertical Paths: The operators `^*` and `^@` enable matching of vertical paths of arbitrary depth. The first, as indicated, requires the existence of a descendant of the specified type, while the second, with arguments such as `(^@ P1 P2 ... Pn)` matches a tree whose root matches `P1`, and has a child matching `P2`, which in turn has a child matching `P3`, and so on. Note that this basic form is indifferent to the point of attachment of each successive offspring to its parent; but we can also specify a point of attachment in any of the `P1`, `P2`, etc., by writing `@` for one of its children. Because this operator (`@`) does not appear outside the vertical path context, it was not listed with the other operators above. Note as well that the argument sequence `P1 P2 ...` can itself be specified as a pattern (e.g., via `(+ ...)`), and in this case there is no advance commitment to the depth of the tree being matched.

Computable Predicates: Arbitrary predicates can be used during the pattern matching process (and consequently the transduction process). Symbols with names ending in a question mark, and with associated function definitions, are interpreted as predicates. When a predicate is encountered during pattern matching, it is called with the current subtree as input. The result is nil or non-nil, and when nil is returned the current match fails, otherwise it succeeds (but the non-nil value is not used further). Additionally, supporting user-defined predicates enables the use of named patterns.

Some Example Patterns: Here are examples of particular patterns, with verbal explanations. Also see Table 1, at the top of the next page, for additional patterns with example bindings.

- `(! (+ A) (+ B))`
  Matches a non-empty sequence of `A`'s or a non-empty sequence of `B`'s, but not a sequence containing both.

- `(* (<> A A))`
  Matches an even number of `A`'s.

- `(B (* (<> B B)))`
  Matches an odd number of `B`'s.

- `(({} A B C))`
  Matches `(A B C)`, `(A C B)`, `(B A C)`, `(B C A)`, `(C A B)` and `(C B A)` and nothing else.

- `((<> A B C))`
  Matches `(A B C)` and nothing else.

- `(^* X)`
  Matches any tree that has descendant `X`.

- `(^@ (+ (@ _*)) X)`
  Matches any tree with leftmost leaf `X`.

Pattern	Tree	Bindings
`_!`	`(A B C)`	`(_! (A B C)`
`(_* F)`	`(A B (C D E) F)`	`(_* A B (C D E))`
`(A B _? F)`	`(A B (C D E) F)`	`(_? (C D E))`
`(A B _? (C D E) F)`	`(A B (C D E) F)`	`(_?)`
`(^@ _! (C _*) E)`	`(A B (C D E) F)`	`(^@ (A B (C D E) F)) (_* D E)`
`(A B (<> (C D E)) F)`	`(A B (C D E) F)`	`(<> (C D E))`
`(A B (<> C D E) F)`	`(A B (C D E) F)`	`nil`

Table 1: Binding Examples

Transductions

Transductions are specified with the transduction operator, `/`, which takes two arguments. The left argument may be any tree pattern and the right argument may be constructed of literals, variables from the lhs pattern, and function calls.

Transductions may be applied to the roots of trees or arbitrary subtrees, and they may be restricted to apply at most once, or until convergence. When applying transductions to arbitrary subtrees, trees are searched top-down, left to right. When a match to the transduction lhs pattern occurs, the resulting bindings and transduction rhs are used to create a new tree, which then replaces the tree (or subtree) that matched the lhs.

Here are a few examples of simple template to template transductions:

- `(/ X Y)`
  Replaces the symbol `X` with the symbol `Y`.
- `(/ (! X Y Z) (A))`
  Replaces any `X`, `Y`, or `Z` with `A`.
- `(/ (! X) (! !))`
  Duplicates an `X`.
- `(/ (X _* Y) (X Y))`
  Remove all subtrees between `X` and `Y`.
- `(/ (_! _* _!1) (_!1 _* _!))`
  Swaps the subtrees on the boundaries.

A transduction operator may appear nested within a composite pattern. The enclosing pattern effectively restricts the context in which the transduction will be applied, because only a match to the entire pattern will trigger a transduction. In this case, the transduction is applied at the location in the tree where it matches. The rhs of such a transduction is allowed to reference the bindings of variables that appear in the enclosing pattern. We call these local transductions, as distinct from replacement of entire trees. Local transductions are especially advantageous when performing vertical path operations, allowing for very concise specifications of local changes. For example, the transduction

```
(^@ (* ((! S SBAR) _+))
    (/ (WH _!)
       (REL-WH (WH _!))))
```

wraps `(REL-WH ...)` around a `(WH ...)` constituent occurring as a descendant of a vertical succession of clausal (`S` or `SBAR`) constituents. Applied to the tree `(S (SBAR (WH X) B) A)`, this yields the new tree `(S (SBAR (REL-WH (WH X)) B) A)`. Additional examples appear later (especially in the parse tree refinement section).

TTT also supports constructive functions, with bound variables as arguments, in the rhs templates, such as `join-with-dash!`, which concatenates all the bound symbols with intervening dashes, and `subst-new!`, which will be discussed later. One can imagine additional functions, such as `reverse!`, `l-shift!`, `r-shift!`, or any other function of a list of terms that may be useful to the application at hand. Symbols with names ending in the exclamation mark are assumed to be associated with function definitions, and when appearing as the first element of a list are executed during output template construction. To avoid writing many near-redundant functions, we use the simple function `apply!` to apply arbitrary Lisp functions during template construction.

Theoretical Properties

A thorough treatment of the formal properties of tree transducers is (Comon, 2007). A good overview of the dimensions of variability among formal tree transducers is given in (Knight, 2007). The main properties are restrictions on the height of the tree fragments allowed in rules, linearity, and whether the rules can delete arbitrary subtrees. Among the more popular and recent ones, synchronous tree substitution grammars (STSG), synchronous tree sequence substitution grammars (STSSG), and multi bottom-up tree transducers (MBOT) constrain their rules to be linear and non-deleting, which is important for efficient rule learning and transduction execution (Chiang, 2004; Galley et. al, 2004; Yamada and Knight, 2001; Zhang et. al, 2008; Maletti, 2010).

The language TTT does not have any such restrictions, as it is intended as a general programming aid, with a concise syntax for potentially radical transformations, rather than a model of particular classes of linguistic operations. Thus, for example, the 5-element pattern `(! ((* A) B) ((* A) C) ((* A) D) ((* A) E) ((* A)))` applied to the expression `(A A A A A)` rescans the latter 5 times, implying quadratic complexity. (Our current implementation does not attempt regular expression reduction for efficient recognition.) With the addition of the permutation operator {}, we can force all permutations of certain patterns to be tried in an unsuccessful match (e.g., `(({} (! A B C) (! A B C) (! A B C)))` applied to `(C B E)`), leading to exponential complexity. (Again, our current implementation does not attempt to optimize.) Also, allowance for repeated application of a set of rules to a tree, until no further applications are possible, leads to Turing equivalence. This of course is true even if only the 4 underscore-operators are allowed: We can simulate the successive transformations of the configurations of a Turing machine with string rewriting rules, which are easily expressed in terms of those operators and `/`. Additionally, pattern predicates and function application in the right-hand sides of rules are features present in TTT that are not included in the above formal models. In themselves (even without iterative rule application), these unrestricted predicates and functions lead to Turing equivalence.

The set of pattern matching operators was chosen so that a number of disparate pattern matching programs could all be replaced with concise TTT rules. It does subsume regular tree expressions and can therefore be used to match any regular tree language. Specifically, alternation can be expressed with `!` and (vertical) iteration with `^@` and `*`. The example expression from (Comon, 2007) can be specified as `(^@ (* (cons 0 @)) nil)`, which matches Lisp expressions corresponding to lists of zero or more zeros. TTT also differs from standard tree automata by lack of an explicit state.

Nondeterminism and noncommutativity: In general, given a set of transductions (or even a single transduction) and an input tree there may be several ways to apply the transductions, resulting in different trees. This phenomenon comes from three sources:

- Rule application order - transductions are not in general commutative.
- Bindings - a pattern may have many sets of consistent bindings to a tree (e.g., pattern `(_* _*1)` can be bound to the tree `(X Y Z)` in four distinct ways).
- Subtree search order - a single transduction may be applicable to a tree in multiple locations (e.g., `(/ _! X)` could replace any node of a tree, including the root, with a single symbol).

Therefore some trees may have many reduced forms with respect to a set of transductions (where by reduced we mean a tree to which no transductions are applicable) and even more reachable forms.

Our current implementation does not attempt to enumerate possible transductions. Rather, for a given tree and a list of transductions, each transduction (in the order given) is applied in top-down fashion at each feasible location (matching the lhs), always using the first binding that results from this depth-first, left-to-right (i.e., pre-order) search. Our assumption is that the typical user has a clear sense of the order in which transformations are to be performed, and is working with rules that do not interact in unexpected ways. For example, consider the cases of PP misattachment mentioned earlier. In most cases, such misattachments are disjoint (e.g., consider a caption reading "John and Mary in front and David and Sue in the back", where both PPs may well have been attached to the proper noun immediately to the left, instead of to the appropriate conjunction). It is also possible for one rule application to change the context of another, but this is not necessarily problematic. For instance, suppose that in the sentence "John drove the speaker to the airport in a hurry" the PP "to the airport" has been misattached to the NP for "the speaker" and that the PP "in a hurry" has been misattached to the NP for "the airport". Suppose further that we have a repair rule that carries a PP attached to an NP upward in the parse tree until it reaches a VP node, reattaching the PP as a child of that VP. (The repair rule might incorporate a computable predicate that detects a poor fit between an NP and a PP that modifies it.) Then the result will be the same regardless of the order in which the two repairs are carried out. The difference is just that with a preorder discipline, the second PP ("in a hurry") will move upward by one step less than if the order is reversed, because the first rule application will have shortened the path to the dominating VP by one step.

In the future it may be worthwhile to implement exhaustive exploration of all possible matches and expression rewrites, as has been done in Mathematica. In general this would call for lazy computation, since the set of rewrites may be an infinite set.

4 Some linguistic examples

Parse Tree Refinement: First, here is a simple transduction to delete empty brackets, which sometimes occur in the Brown corpus: `(/ (_* () _*1) (_* _*1))`.

To distinguish between past and passive participles, we want to search for the verb *have*, and change the participle token correspondingly, as discussed earlier. The next two transductions are equivalent – the first is global and the second is an example of a local or on-the-fly transduction. For simplicity we consider only the *has* form of *have*. Observe the more concise form, and simpler variable specifications of the second transduction.

```
(/ (VP _* (VBZ HAS) _*1 (VBN _!) _*2)
   (VP _* (VBZ HAS) _*1 (VBEN _!) _*2))
```

```
(VP _* (VBZ HAS) _* ((/ VBN VBEN) _!) _*)
```

To distinguish temporal and non-temporal nominals, we use a computable predicate to detect temporal nouns, and then annotate the NP tag accordingly. (One more time, we show global and local variants.)

```
(/ (NP _* nn-temporal?)
    (NP-TIME _* nn-temporal?))
((/ NP NP-TIME) _* nn-temporal?)
```

Assimilation of verb particles into single constituents is useful to semantic interpretation, and is accomplished with the transduction:

```
(/ (VP (VB \_!1)
       (\{\} (PRT (RP _!2)) (NP _*1)))
   (VP (VB _!1 _!2)  (NP _*1)))
```

We often particularize PPs to show the preposition involved, e.g., PP-OF, PP-FROM, etc. Note that this transduction uses the `join-with-dash!` function, which enables us to avoid writing a separate transduction for each preposition:

```
(/ (PP (IN _!)  _*1)
    ((join-with-dash! PP _!)
     (IN _!)  _*1))
```

Such a rule transforms subtrees such as `(PP (IN FROM))` by rewriting the PP tag as `(PP-FROM (IN FROM))`.

As a final syntactic processing example (transitioning to discourse phenomena and semantics), we illustrate the use of TTT in establishing potential coreferents licensed by C-command relations, for the sentence mentioned earlier. We assume that for reference purposes, NP nodes are decorated with a SEM-INDEX feature (with an integer value), and pronominal NPs are in addition decorated with a CANDIDATE-COREF feature, whose value is a list of indices (initially empty). Thus we have the following parse structure for the sentence at issue (where for understandabilty of the relatively complex parse tree we depart from Treebank conventions not only in the use of some explicit features but also in using linguistically more conventional phrasal and part-of-speech category names; R stands for relative clause):

```
(S ((NP SEM-INDEX 1) (NAME John))
   (VP (V shows)
       ((NP SEM-INDEX 2) (NAME Lillian))
       ((NP SEM-INDEX 3) (DET the)
        (N (N snowman)
           (R (RELPRON that)
              ((S GAP NP)
               ((NP SEM-INDEX 4
                 CANDIDATE-COREF ())
                (PRON he))
               ((VP GAP NP) (V built)
                ((NP SEM-INDEX 4)
                 (PRON *trace*)))))))))
```

Here is a TTT rule that adjoins the index of a C-commanding NP node to the CANDIDATE-COREF list of a C-commanded pronominal NP:

```
(_* ((NP _* SEM-INDEX _!. _*) _+) _*
```

```
(^* ((NP _* CANDIDATE-COREF
  (/ _!(adjoin! _!. _!)) _*) (PRON _!))) _*)
```

The NP on the first line is the C-commanding NP, and note that we are using a sticky variable '_!.' for its index, since we need to use it later. (None of the other match variables need to be sticky, and we reuse '_*' and '_!' multiple times.) The key to understanding the rule is the constituent headed by '^*', which triggers a search for a (right) sibling or descendant of a sibling of the NP node that reaches an NP consisting of a pronoun, and thus bearing the CANDIDATE-COREF feature. This feature is replaced "on the fly" by adjoining the index of the C-commanding node (the value of '_!.') to it. For the sample tree, the result is the following (note the value '(1)' of the CANDIDATE-COREF list):

```
(S ((NP SEM-INDEX 1) (NAME John))
   (VP (V shows)
       ((NP SEM-INDEX 2) (NAME Lillian))
       ((NP SEM-INDEX 3) (DET the)
        (N (N snowman)
           (R (RELPRON that)
              ((S GAP NP)
               ((NP SEM-INDEX 4
                 CANDIDATE-COREF (1))
                (PRON he))
               ((VP GAP NP) (V built)
                ((NP SEM-INDEX 4)
                 (PRON *trace*))))))))))
```

Of course, this does not yet incorporate number and gender checks, but while these could be included, it is preferable to gather candidates and heuristically pare them down later. Thus repeated application of the rule would also add the index 2 (for *Lillian*) to CANDIDATE-COREF.

Working with Logical Forms

Skolemization: Skolemization of an existential formula of type (some x R S), where x is a variable, R is a restrictor formula and S is the nuclear scope, is performed via the transduction

```
(/ (some _! _!1 _!2)
   (subst-new! _! (_!1 and.cc _!2))).
```

The function subst-new! replaces all occurrences of a free variable symbol in an expression with a new one. (We assume that no variable occurs both bound and free in the same expression.) It uses a TTT transduction to accomplish this. For example, (some x (x politician.n) (x honest.a)) becomes ((C1.skol politician.n) and.cc (C1.skol honest.a)).

Inference: We can use the following rule to accomplish simple default inferences such as that if most things with property P have property Q, and most things with property Q have property R, then (in the absence of knowledge to the contrary) many things with property P also have property R. (Our logical forms use infix syntax for predication, i.e., the predicate follows the "subject" argument. Predicates can be lambda abstracts, and the computable boolean function pred? checks for arbitrary predicative constructs.)

```
(/
 (_* (most _!.1
       (_!.1 (!.p pred?))
       (_!.1 (!.q pred?)))
  _* (most _!.2
       (_!.2 !.q)
       (_!.2 (!.r pred?))) _*)
 (many _!.1 (_!.1 !.p) (_!.1 !.r)))
```

For example, ((most x (x dog.n) (x pet.n)) (most y (y pet.n) (x friendly.a))) yields the default inference (many (x dog.n) (x friendly.a)).

The assumption here is that the two *most*-formulas are embedded in a list of formulas (selected by the inference algorithm), and the three occurrences of _* allow for miscellaneous surrounding formulas. (To allow for arbitrary ordering of formulas in the working set, we also provide a variant with the two *most*-formulas in reverse order.) Inference with tree transduction rules has also been performed by (Koller and Stefan, 2010).

Predicate Disambiguation: The following rules are applicable to patterns of predication such as ((det dog.n have.v (det tail.n)), ((det bird.n have.v (det nest.n)), and ((det man.n) have.v (det accident.n)). (Think of det as an unspecified, unscoped quantifier.) The rules simultaneously introduce plausible patterns of quantification and plausible disambiguations of the various senses of have.v (e.g., have as part, possess, eat, experience):

```
(/ ((det (! animal?)) have.v
    (det (!1 animal-part?)))
   (all-or-most x (x !)
    (some e ((pair x e) enduring)
     (some y (y !1)
      ((x have-as-part.v y) ** e)))))

(/ ((det (! agent?)) have.v
    (det (!1 possession?)))
   (many x (x !)
    (some e
     (some y (y !1)
      (x possess.v y) ** e))))
```

```
(/ ((det (! animal?)) have.v
    (det (!1 food?)))
   (many x (x !)
    (occasional e
     (some y (y !1)
      (x eat.v y) ** e))))

(/ ((det (! person?)) have.v
    (det (!1 event?)))
   (many x (x !)
    (occasional e
     (some y (y !1)
      ((x experience.v y) ** e)))))
```

Computable predicates such as `animal?` and `event?` are evaluated with the help of WordNet and other resources. Details of the logical form need not concern us, but it should be noted that the '`**`' connects sentences to events they characterize much as in various other theories of events and situations.

Thus, for example, `((det dog.n have.v (det tail.n))` is mapped to:

```
(all-or-most x (x dog.n
 (some e ((pair x e) enduring)
  (some y (y tail.n)
   ((x have-as-part.v y) ** e)))))
```

This expresses that for all or most dogs, the dog has an enduring attribute (formalized as an agent-event pair) of having a tail as a part.

Logical Interpretation: The following transductions directly map some simple parse trees to logical forms. The rules, applied as often as possible to a parse tree, replace all syntactic constructs, recognizable from (Treebank-style) phrase headers like `(JJ ...)`, `(NP ...)`, `(VP ...)`, `(S ...)`, etc., by corresponding semantic constructs. For example, "The dog bit John Doe", parsed as

```
(S (NP (DT the) (NN dog))
   (VP (VBD bit)
       (NP (NNP John) (NNP Doe))))
```

yields `(the x (x dog.n) (x bit.v John_Doe.name))`.

Type-extensions such as '`.a`', '`.n`', and '`.v`' indicate adjectival, nominal, and verbal predicates, and the extension '`.name`' indicates an individual constant (name); these are added by the functions `make-adj!`, `make-noun!`, and so on. The fourth rule below combines two successive proper nouns (NNPs) into one. We omit event variables, tense and other refinements.

```
(/ (JJ _!)  (make-adj! _!))
(/ (NN _!)  (make-noun! _!))
(/ (VBD _!)  (make-verb! _!))
(/ (_*.a (NNP _!.1) (NNP _!.2) _*.b)
   (_*.a (NNP _!.1 _!.2) _*.b))
(/ (NNP _+) (make-name! (_+)))
(/ (NP _!)  _!)
(/ (S (NP (DT the) _!)  (VP _+))
(the x (x _!)  (x _+))
```

These rules are illustrative only, and are not fully compositional, as they interpret an NP with a determiner only in the context of a sentential subject, and a VP only in the context of a sentential predicate. Also, by scoping the variable of quantification, they do too much work at once. A more general approach would use compositional rules such as `(/ (S (!1 NP?) (!2 VP?)) ((sem! !1) (sem! !2)))`, where the `sem!` function again makes use of TTT, recursively unwinding the semantics, with rules like the first five above providing lexical-level `sem!-values`.

We have also experimented with rendering logical forms back into English, which is rather easier, mainly requiring dropping of variables and brackets and some reshuffling of constituents.

5 Conclusion

The TTT language is well-suited to the applications it was aimed at, and is already proving useful in current syntactic/semantic applications. It provides a very concise, transparent way of specifying transformations that previously required extensive symbolic processing. Some remaining issues are efficient access to, and deployment of, rules that are locally relevant to a transduction; and heuristics for executing matches and transductions more efficiently (e.g., recognizing various cases where a complex rule cannot possibly match a given tree, because the tree lacks some constituents called for by the rule; or use of efficient methods for matching regular-expression subpatterns).

The language also holds promise for rule-learning, thanks to its simple template-to-template basic syntax. The kinds of learning envisioned are learning parse-tree repair rules, and perhaps also LF repair rules and LF-to-English rules.

Acknowledgments

The work was supported by ONR-STTR award N00014-11-10417, and NSF grants IIS-1016735, NSF IIS-0916599, and NSF IIS-0910611.

References

Eugene Charniak and Mark Johnson. 2005. Coarse-to-Fine n-Best Parsing and MaxEnt Discriminative Reranking. ACL 2005, 173–180. Association for Computational Linguistics, Ann Arbor, MI, USA.

David Chiang. 2004. Evaluation of Grammar Formalisms for Applications to Natural Language Processing and Biological Sequence Analysis. Phd. Thesis. University of Pennsylvania.

H. Comon and M. Dauchet and R. Gilleron and C. Löding and F. Jacquemard and D. Lugiez and S. Tison and M. Tommasi 2007. Tree Automata Techniques and Applications Available on: http://www.grappa.univ-lille3.fr/tata

Michel Galley and Mark Hopkins and Kevin Knight and Daniel Marcu 2004. What's in a Translation Rule?. NAACL 2004, 273–280. Boston, MA, USA.

Thomas Genet and Valerie View Triem Tong 2003. Timbuk: A Tree Automata Library http://www.irisa.fr/celtique/genet/timbuk/

Ralph Griswold 1971. *The SNOBOL4 Programming Language*. Prentice-Hall, Inc. Upper Saddle River, NJ, USA.

Paul Hudak, John Peterson, and Joseph Fasel. 2000. A Gentle Introduction To Haskell: Version 98. Los Alamos National Laboratory. http://www.haskell.org/tutorial/patterns.html.

Alexander Koller and Stefan Thater. 2010. Computing weakest readings. ACL 2010. 30–39. Stroudsburg, PA, USA.

Kevin Knight. 2007. Capturing practical natural language transformations. *Machine Translation*, Vol 21, Issue 2, 121–133. Kluwer Academic Publishers. Hingham, MA, USA.

Roger Levy and Galen Andrew 2006. Tregex and Tsurgeon: tools for querying and manipulating tree data structures. *Language Resources Evaluation Conference* (LREC '06).

Andreas Maletti 2010. Why synchronous tree substitution grammars?. HLT 2010. Association for Computational Linguistics, Stroudsburg, PA, USA.

Jonathan May and Kevin Knight 2008 A Primer on Tree Automata Software for Natural Language Processing. http://www.isi.edu/licensed-sw/tiburon/

Peter Norvig 1991. *Paradigms of Artificial Intelligence Programming* Morgan Kaufmann. Waltham, MA, USA.

Don Rozenberg 2002. SnoPy - Snobol Pattern Matching Extension for Python. http://snopy.sourceforge.net/user-guide.html.

Wolfram Research, Inc. 2010. *Wolfram Mathematica 8 Documentation*. Champagne, IL, USA. http://reference.wolfram.com/mathematica/guide/RulesAndPatterns.html.

World Wide Web Consortium. 1999. XML Path Language (XPath) http://www.w3.org/TR/xpath/

1999. XSL Transformations (XSLT) http://www.w3.org/TR/xslt

Kenji Yamada and Kevin Knight 2001. A Syntax-Based Statistical Translation Model. ACL 2001, 523–530. Stroudsburg, PA, USA.

Min Zhang and Hongfei Jiang and Aiti Aw and Haizhou Li and Chew Lim Tan and Sheng Li 2008. A tree sequence alignment-based tree-to-tree translation model. ACL 2008.

Second position clitics and monadic second-order transduction

Neil Ashton
203 Morrill Hall
Cornell University
Ithaca, NY 14853-4701
nma38@cornell.edu

Abstract

The simultaneously phonological and syntactic grammar of second position clitics is an instance of the broader problem of applying constraints across multiple levels of linguistic analysis. Syntax frameworks extended with simple tree transductions can make efficient use of these necessary additional forms of structure. An analysis of Sahidic Coptic second position clitics in a context-free grammar extended by a monadic second-order transduction exemplifies this approach.

1 Introduction

Second position (2P) clitics are ubiquitous in the world's languages, found in genetically and typologically diverse languages (e.g. Serbo-Croatian, Warlpiri, O'odham) from all documented periods (e.g. Hittite, spoken ca. 1600–1300 BC). They present a persistent challenge for syntactic analysis, inducing a peculiar form of crossing dependency which is not easily expressed in any standard restrictive grammar framework.

2P clitics are emblematic of a wider class of problematic phenomena which existing frameworks can address by incorporating a notion of prosodic constituency. The transductive perspective on mildly context-sensitive grammar formalisms, which treats them as monadic second-order transductions of regular tree languages, suggests how this can be done: by transducing prosodic constituency from syntactic phrase structure.

The prosodic conditioning of 2P clisis is particularly salient in Sahidic Coptic (Reintges, 2004).[1] A context-free phrase structure grammar extended by a monadic second-order transduction is able to make use of the phonological structure necessary to give a linguistically plausible analysis to a fragment of Coptic clitic syntax.

2 Second position clitics and prosodic constituency

2.1 Second position

An intuitive account of the syntax of 2P clitics[2] has been known since Wackernagel (1892). The 2P clitic, which is an immediate functional dependent of a clause, e.g. a sentential adverb, discourse particle, pronominal argument, etc., appears after the *first word* of that clause, potentially interrupting whatever constituent contains that word as its leftmost member, as the chain of 2P clitics interrupts the NP in the following Serbo-Croatian sentence.[3]

(1) [*Taj* <u>*=joj=ga=je*</u> *čovek*]$_{NP}$ *poklonio.*
that =her=it=AUX man presented
'That man presented her with it.' (Bögel et al., 2010)

[1] "Coptic" refers to the latest form of the Egyptian language. Sahidic Coptic, the major literary dialect of Coptic from the 4th to the 10th centuries AD, is survived by a rich corpus of Greek-alphabet texts. The only extant computational model of Sahidic Coptic grammar is apparently that of Orlandi (2004). This work is unfortunately not available to the author, and so no comparison of approaches has been possible.

[2] A "clitic" is, descriptively, a word-like element with affix-like phonological dependence ("clisis") on other words. Proclitics and enclitics are dependent on right- and left-adjacent words, respectively, and 2P clitics are a special case of enclitics. For more on clitics, see Zwicky (1977), Aikhenvald (2003), and Anderson (2005).

[3] Clitic boundaries are marked with an equals sign, after the Leipzig glossing conventions.

This constituency-breaking word order pattern alone poses a descriptive challenge. The difficulty is exacerbated by the fact that the "word" targeted by the 2P clitic is not in general syntactically characterizable. It is rather a phonological constituent that may include incorporated clitics (Inkelas and Zec, 1990; Zec, 2005). The alternation in the position of the 2P clitic *de* in the Coptic sentences (2) and (3) illustrates this well.

(2) *a=t=ef=sone* <u>*=de*</u> *ol*
AUX.PF=the=3SG=sister =and gather
en=n=ef=kees
ACC=the=3SG=bones
'and his sister gathered his bones' (Mena, Martyrd. 4a:1-2)

(3) *a=w=tamio* <u>*=de*</u> *en=u=taive*
AUX.PF=3PL=make =and ACC=a=coffin
'and they made a coffin' (Mena, Martyrd. 5a:27-28)

In both sentences, *de* functions as a clausal conjunction. But its position varies, appearing between the main verb and its subject in (2) and between the verb and its object in (3). This alternation is most plausibly phonological. The 2P clitic appears after the first independently pronounceable word, including its attached clitics, such as the pronominal subject *w-* in (3) and the tense auxiliary *a-* in both sentences. The behavior of 2P clitics when the verb itself or its direct object are clitics is consistent with this analysis.

Phonological properties alone, however, do not suffice to describe the syntax of 2P clitics. They are constrained to appear within a syntactically determined subpart of their host clause, typically ignoring topicalized or otherwise left-dislocated elements and thus appearing quite far from strict phonological second position. Describing 2P clisis thus requires reference to both syntactic and phonological structure.

2.2 Prosodic constituency via tree transduction

The notion of prosodic constituency (Nespor and Vogel, 1986; Selkirk, 1986) provides the key to a perspicuous account of the multiple factors at play in the grammar of 2P clitics. Prosodic constituency is a tree structure that defines the "words" and "phrases" relevant to phonology, which are in general distinct from yet closely related to their syntactic equivalents.

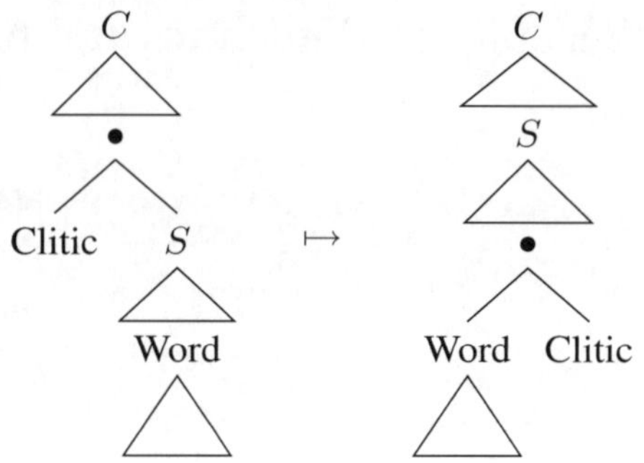

Figure 1: Lowering 2P clitics.

Both the distinctness of and the relationship between syntactic and prosodic constituency can be captured by transducing the latter from the former. This transduction in effect interprets syntactic trees as terms over a signature of phonological operations and normalizes the result. The yield function is a prosodically naive example of such a transduction.

Once this independently necessary transduction has been taken into account, the syntax of 2P clitics is straightforward. The 2P clitic simply has a non-concatenative mode of phonological combination. The clitic and its host clause are siblings in syntactic constituency, and their parent node is interpreted as an operation that wraps the latter around the former—alternatively, lowers the former into the latter.

This analysis, which captures in essence both the "wrapping" (Bach, 1987) and "prosodic inversion" (Halpern, 1995) analyses of 2P clitics, can be schematized as in Figure 1, where "Word" is constrained to be the leftmost node with that label in S.

This transduction is not direction-preserving in the sense of Bloem and Engelfriet (2000): assuming that the clitic crosses unboundedly many nodes on the way to its host word, a crossing dependency is induced in the paths of the target tree. This rules out the possibility of formalizing this analysis by means of popular automaton models such as multi bottom-up tree transducers (Fülöp et al., 2004) or their extended variant (Engelfriet et al., 2009), which cannot describe such dependencies (Maletti, 2011).

The more powerful automata that can be specified using monadic second-order logic (MSO), which include syntactically restricted classes of macro tree transducers (Engelfriet and Maneth, 1999) and deterministic tree-walking transducers (Bloem and Engelfriet, 2000), can perform this transduction. Section 3 defines the transduction in MSO, and Section 4 reflects briefly on its implementation.

3 Sahidic Coptic 2P clitics via CFG+MST

The following context-free grammar and sequence of MSO transductions formalizes, for a fragment of Sahidic Coptic, the analysis of 2P clisis sketched in Section 2.2.

Section 3 breaks the interpretation of a syntactic parse tree as a phonological term into a series ($f_1 - f_7$) of simple composed MSO transductions. A "redex" phonological term is derived (Section 3.3), and its reducible subterms are then evaluated separately (Section 3.4). An algorithmic implementation of the transduction is sketched in Section 3.5.

3.1 Formal preliminaries

The following definitions and assertions rehearse material from Courcelle and Engelfriet (2012), which should be consulted for full details.

3.1.1 Relational structures and tree graphs

A relational signature is a finite set R of relation symbols with associated arity $\rho(r) \in \mathbb{N}^*$ for each $r \in R$. A relational structure over R is a tuple $\mathscr{R} = \langle D_{\mathscr{R}}, (r_{\mathscr{R}})_{r \in R} \rangle$, where $D_{\mathscr{R}}$ is a finite domain of entities and $r_{\mathscr{R}}$, for each $r \in R$, is a $\rho(r)$-ary relation on $D_{\mathscr{R}}$.

A bijection exists between binary relational structures and labelled graphs, with unary and binary relations corresponding to node and edge labels, respectively. Ordered binary trees can be represented as labelled directed graphs, and hence as relational structures, in the obvious way.

3.1.2 Monadic second-order logic

The monadic second-order (MSO) formulas over a relational signature R are as first-order predicate logic, with the addition of monadic second-order variables $X, Y, X', \ldots$ denoting sets of entities, second-order quantification, and a primitive operator for set membership. The substitution of n free variables in a formula ϕ by entities $d_1, \ldots, d_n$ is written $\phi(d_1, \ldots, d_n)$.

An MSO formula over R is interpreted in a relational signature over R. A formula with no free variables is called a sentence. If a sentence ψ is true in a relational structure $\mathscr{R}$, we write $\mathscr{R} \models \psi$, pronounced "$\mathscr{R}$ models ψ".

3.1.3 MSO transduction

An MSO transduction defines a relational structure in terms of another by taking a finite number of copies of nodes from the source domain, keeping those that satisfy particular formulas in the source structure, and defining the relations that hold in the target structure by means of formulas modeled by the source structure. The generalization of MSO transduction to k-copying MSO transduction (Courcelle, 1991) allows the target domain to be larger than its source. MSO transductions whose formulas do not refer to parameters define deterministic functions.

A (parameterless, k-copying) MSO transduction over a relational signature R is specified by a triple $\langle k, \Delta, \Theta \rangle$, where $k \in \mathbb{N}$ and $\Delta = \{\delta_i \mid 0 \leq i \leq k\}$ and $\Theta = \{\theta_w \mid w \in W\}$ are sets of MSO formulas with free variables, and W is the set of all tuples $(r, i_1, \ldots, i_{\rho(r)})$ for $r \in R$. This triple is called a definition scheme.

A definition scheme specifies a target relational structure T with respect to a source relational structure S as follows. The domain D_T of T is the set $(D_0 \times \{0\}) \cup \ldots \cup (D_k \times \{k\})$, where each $D_i = \{d \in D_S \mid S \models \delta_i(d)\}$. For each n-ary relation r in the relational signature of T, an n-ary relation on D_T is defined as:

$$\bigcup_{i_0,\ldots,i_n \in [k]} \begin{array}{l} \{((d_0, i_0), \ldots, (d_n, i_n)) \mid \\ \quad d_0 \in D_{i_0}, \ldots, d_n \in D_{i_n}, \\ \quad S \models \theta_{r,i_0,\ldots,i_n}(d_0, \ldots, d_n)\} \end{array}$$

Intuitively, a formula δ_i specifies conditions on the existence of the ith copy of a node in the target structure. A formula $\theta_{(r,i_0,\ldots,j_{\rho(r)})}$ specifies conditions on the relation r holding between copies of nodes indexed $i, \ldots, j$ in the target structure.

3.2 Definitions and abbreviations

3.2.1 Base CFG

The phrase structure grammar which serves as the basis of the analysis of Coptic is presented in

$S \rightarrow Cl\ S'$	$NP_{pro} \rightarrow Pro$
$S' \rightarrow Aux\ VP$	$NP_N \rightarrow Det^{sg}_{fem}\ N'^{sg}_{fem}$
$VP \rightarrow NP_N\ V'$	$NP_N \rightarrow Det_{indef}\ N^{sg}_{fem}$
$VP \rightarrow NP_{pro}\ V'$	$NP_N \rightarrow Det^{pl}\ N'^{pl}$
$V' \rightarrow V\ AccP$	$N'^{sg}_{fem} \rightarrow NP_{pro}\ N^{sg}_{fem}$
$Cl \rightarrow$ de	$N'^{pl} \rightarrow NP_{pro}\ N^{pl}$
$Aux \rightarrow$ a	$AccP \rightarrow Acc_N\ NP_N$
$V \rightarrow$ ol $\mid$ tamio	$AccP \rightarrow Acc_{pro}\ NP_{pro}$
$N^{sg}_{fem} \rightarrow$ sone $\mid$ taive	$Det^{sg}_{fem} \rightarrow$ t
$N^{pl} \rightarrow$ kees	$Det^{pl} \rightarrow$ n
$Acc_N \rightarrow$ en	$Det_{indef} \rightarrow$ u
$Acc_{pro} \rightarrow$ mmo	$Pro \rightarrow$ w $\mid$ ef

Figure 2: Base CFG fragment of Coptic.

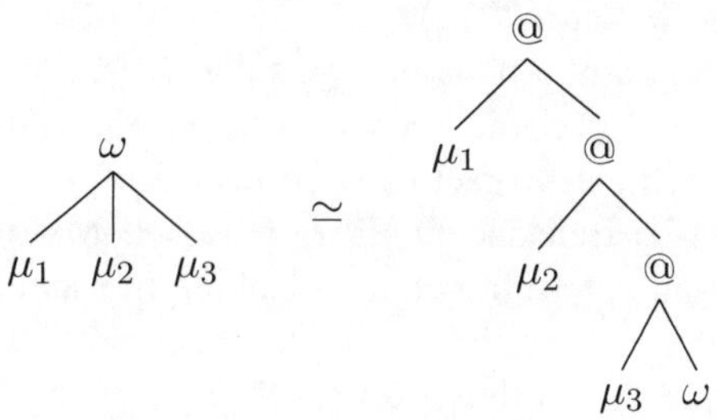

Figure 3: Encoding of n-ary trees.

$\frown$	concatenation
$\bullet_p$	proclisis
$\bullet_e$	enclisis
$\bullet_{2p}$	2P clisis
$\bullet_{id}$	identity
ω	prosodic word
@	extension operator

Table 1: Interpretation of labels.

Figure 2. Its parse trees define a recognizable language of binary trees, members of which can be represented as relational structures, as explained in Section 3.1.1. This CFG fragment, in combination with the transductions detailed below, suffices to generate sentences (2) and (3) from Section 2.1.

This grammar encodes several claims, already alluded to in Section 2.1, about the syntactic structure of Coptic. Syntactic dependencies are represented by constituency in the usual way. The immediate dependence of the 2P clitic *de* on a host clause is expressed by the siblinghood of *Cl* and *S'* under *S*.

Features of lexical items relevant for agreement and allomorphy are encoded as diacritics on nonterminals, allowing determiners to agree with nouns in gender and the accusative case preposition to covary with the nominal or pronominal status of its complement.

3.2.2 Encoding of nodes with unbounded branching

Syntactic trees are interpreted into prosodic trees, which may contain prosodic word constituents that branch unboundedly wide. To fix a binary encoding for such constituents, a "*cons* cell"-like variant of the extension operator encoding (Comon et al., 2007, p. 210) is adopted, in which a term of the form $@(x, y)$ is interpreted as extending the interpretation of y by adding x to its root as its leftmost child. An example of this encoding is given in Figure 3.

Only the fragment of prosodic constituency relevant to the alternation shown in sentences (2) and (3) is derived. The output tree therefore contains operator-encoded prosodic constituents as subtrees of *unencoded* trees containing unanalyzed phonological combination operators.

3.2.3 Relational signature and abbreviations

All MSO transductions presented below are defined over a binary relational signature $R = R_1 \cup R_2$. The set of node labels R_1 is given by the union of the set of all non-terminal and terminal node names in the grammar of Figure 2 and the set $\{\frown, \bullet_p, \bullet_e, \bullet_{2p}, \bullet_{id}, \omega, @\}$. The interpretation of these predicates is given in Table 1. The set of binary predicates R_2 is simply $\{\triangleleft_0, \triangleleft_1\}$, the left and right child relations, written as infix operators as a notational convenience.

It will be useful to define several new binary predicates as syntactic abbreviations. I assume reflexive and irreflexive transitive closures r^* and r^+ of relations $r \in R_2$, as well as immediate domination and precedence $\triangleleft, \prec$, as abbreviations of MSO formulas over primitive predicates.[4]

Recurring structural properties of lexical items in the base CFG are given by the unary syntactic abbreviations defined below.[5] These include pro-

[4]On the MSO-definability of these, see Courcelle and Engelfriet (2012).

[5]"$\psi := \phi$" is to be read "ψ is an abbreviation for ϕ".

clitic and 2P clitic status ($Pc(x)$, $2P(x)$), independent pronounceability ($Str(x)$), and the property of being a leaf ($Leaf(x)$).

$$\begin{aligned} Pc(x) &:= \mathrm{a}(x) \vee \mathrm{en}(x) \vee \mathrm{t}(x) \vee \mathrm{n}(x) \\ 2P(x) &:= \mathrm{de}(x) \\ Str(x) &:= \mathrm{ol}(x) \vee \mathrm{sone}(x) \\ &\qquad \vee \mathrm{kees}(x) \vee \mathrm{mmo}(x) \\ Leaf(x) &:= \mathrm{de}(x) \vee \mathrm{a}(x) \vee \ldots \end{aligned}$$

MSO transductions are given by transduction schemes, as defined in Section 3.1.3. In the case that $k = 0$, irrelevant subscripts are omitted. Unless otherwise specified, all formulas δ_i can be assumed to be the constant *True*.

3.3 Transducing a reducible term

A syntactic constituency tree can be interpreted as a term in a phonological algebra, with non-leaf nodes interpreted as operations effecting phonological combination in various modes. Pronounceable utterances, which consist of concatenations of prosodic constituents (i.e. terms over leaves from the base CFG, @, ω, and $\frown$), are normal forms.

This complex interpretation is broken into smaller transductions, the first set of which lays the foundation for the reduction of the "clitic" modes of combination. Non-leaf nodes are first replaced by appropriate combination operators (Section 3.3.1). Unary nodes are then eliminated (Section 3.3.2). Finally, the prosodic structure necessary for the next phase of interpretation is generated (Section 3.3.3).

3.3.1 Relabeling

Non-terminal leaves in the syntactic tree are replaced by operators indicating modes of phonological combination, as presented in Table 1.

The transduction to unreduced phonological terms is sensitive to the structure of the syntactic tree. Some leaves, e.g. clitic pronouns, are not strictly proclitic or enclitic but vary by context: the pronominal subject of a verb or possessor of a noun is proclitic, whereas the pronominal complement of an accusative preposition or pronoun-selecting verb is enclitic. The relevant syntactic context is the child status of NP_{pro} nodes. Hence the parent of an NP_{pro} node is replaced by $\bullet_p$ if NP_{pro} is its left child, by $\bullet_e$ if NP_{pro} its right child.

All non-pronominal clitics are phonologically combined with the sibling of their phonologically vacuous unary parent node. Thus the grandparents of all such clitic leaves are replaced by the appropriate clitic combination operator, $\bullet_p$ for proclitics and $\bullet_{2p}$ for 2P clitics. Unary nodes are replaced by $\bullet_{id}$, and all other non-leaf nodes are replaced by $\frown$. Leaf node labels are left unchanged.

The definition scheme $f_1 = \langle 0, \Delta, \Theta \rangle$, where Θ is defined as the union of the formulas given below, specifies this transduction. The body of the $\theta_\frown$ formula, which consists largely of the disjunction of the negations of the preceding formulas, is omitted, as signaled by $[etc]$; and the θ_w formula which reasserts leaf labels is omitted altogether.

$$\begin{aligned} \theta_{\bullet_e}(x) &= \exists x'(NP_{pro}(x') \wedge x \lhd_1 x') \\ \theta_{\bullet_p}(x) &= \exists x'(NP_{pro}(x') \wedge x \lhd_0 x') \\ &\quad \vee \exists x', x''(x \lhd_0 x' \wedge x' \lhd_0 x'' \wedge Pc(x'')) \\ \theta_{\bullet_{2p}}(x) &= \exists x', x''(x \lhd_0 x' \wedge x' \lhd_0 x'' \wedge 2P(x'')) \\ \theta_{\bullet_{id}}(x) &= \exists x'(x \lhd_0 x') \wedge \neg \exists x''(x \lhd_1 x'') \\ \theta_\frown(x) &= [etc] \end{aligned}$$

3.3.2 Eliminating unary nodes

Before any further interpretation takes place, unary $\bullet_{id}$ nodes, which are phonologically vacuous, can be eliminated.

The definition scheme $f_2 = \langle 0, \Delta, \Theta \rangle$, with Θ defined as the union of the following formulas (for $i \in \{0, 1\}$), eliminates unary nodes by connecting a non-$\bullet_{id}$ node dominated by a path of $\bullet_{id}$ nodes to the parent of the topmost $\bullet_{id}$ in the path. Again, $[etc]$ stands for the omitted "elsewhere condition", which here reasserts edges from the source.

$$\begin{aligned} \theta_{\lhd_i}(x, y) = \neg \bullet_{id}(x) \wedge \neg \bullet_{id}(y) \\ \wedge \exists x'(x \lhd_i x' \wedge x' \lhd^+ y \\ \wedge \forall y'(x' \lhd^* y' \wedge y' \lhd^+ y \\ \rightarrow \bullet_{id}(y'))) \vee [etc] \end{aligned}$$

An example of the composed transduction $f_2 \circ f_1$ is given in Figure 4.

3.3.3 Base prosodic words

Before reducing the remaining reducible modes of combination, it is necessary to create prosodic word constituents, notated ω, that cover the independently pronounceable "strong" leaves of the tree, allowing the word-sensitive clitic modes of combination to be interpreted correctly. Prosodic

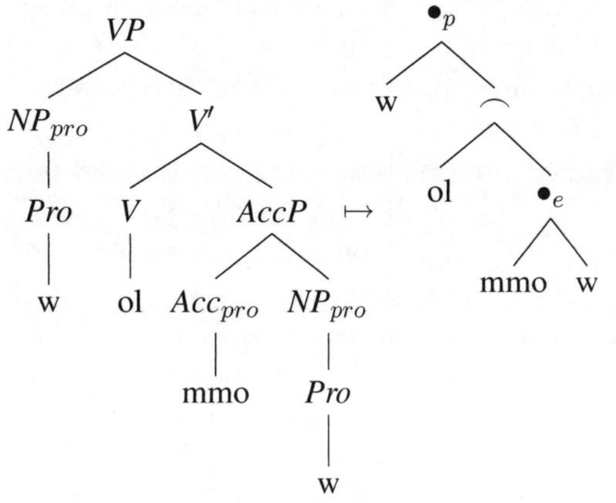

Figure 4: Relabeling and $\bullet_{id}$-elimination.

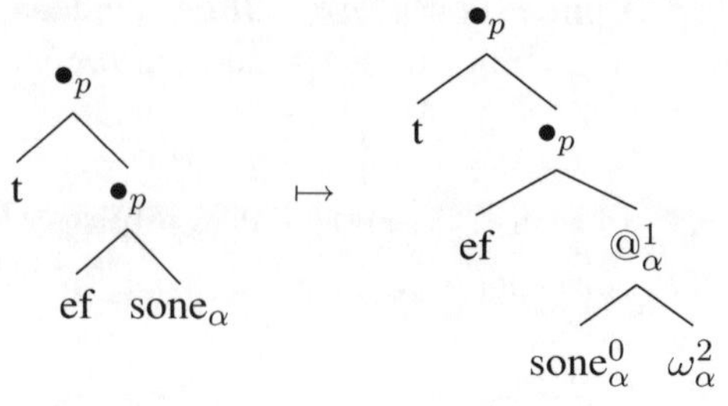

Figure 5: Prosodic word insertion.

words are encoded by the scheme given in Section 3.2.

The definition scheme $f_3 = \langle 2, \Delta, \Theta \rangle$, with Δ and Θ the union of the δ and θ formulas below, specifies a transduction that takes two additional copies of all nodes, relabels the copies of strong leaf nodes as @ and ω, and draws edges as appropriate.

$$
\begin{aligned}
\delta_1(x) = \delta_2(x) &= \\
\theta_{(@,1)}(x) = \theta_{(\omega,2)}(x) &= Str(x) \\
\theta_{(\lhd_1,0,0)}(x,y) &= \neg Str(y) \wedge x \lhd_1 y \\
\theta_{(\lhd_1,0,1)}(x,y) &= Str(y) \wedge x \lhd_1 y \\
\theta_{(\lhd_0,1,0)}(x,y) &= \\
\theta_{(\lhd_1,1,2)}(x,y) &= Str(x) \wedge x = y \\
\theta_{(\lhd_0,0,0)}(x,y) &= True
\end{aligned}
$$

An example of the tree transduction given by f_3 is shown in Figure 5, with identity of copies indicated by subscript letters and the number of the copy by superscript numerals.

3.4 Interpreting clitic combination modes

The composed transduction $f_3 \circ f_2 \circ f_1$ produces reducible phonological terms in which the prosodic structure necessary to interpret the clitic modes of combination ($\bullet_p$, $\bullet_e$, and $\bullet_{2p}$) is present.

The interpretation of the clitic modes proceeds in three steps. "Local" clitics, siblings of prosodic words, are amalgamated into their hosts (Section 3.4.1). "Long-distance" clitics, which are not thus locally attached, are lowered to their hosts (Section 3.4.2) and then attached as local clitics. Second-position clitics are finally lowered and attached by the same means, as a special case (Section 3.4.3).

3.4.1 Local clisis

Locally connected clitics can be directly incorporated into their hosts. The word constituent so derived is the recursive structure (e.g. $[_\omega clitic\ [_\omega host]]$) generally assumed for cliticized words (cf. Inkelas and Zec, 1990; Zec, 2005).

Proclitics and enclitics can be interpreted separately. For proclitics, the relevant notion of "locality" can be expressed by a predicate $\circ_p(x)$, which identifies $\bullet_p$ nodes connected to @ nodes by a path of $\bullet_p$ nodes.

$$
\begin{aligned}
\circ_p(x) := \bullet_p(x) \wedge \exists y(@(y) \\
\wedge\, x \lhd_1^+ y \wedge \forall z(x \lhd^* z \\
\wedge\, z \lhd^+ y \rightarrow \bullet_p(x)))
\end{aligned}
$$

The 2-copying MS transduction specified by the definition scheme $f_4 = \langle 2, \Delta, \Theta \rangle$, with Δ and Θ given by the union of the δ and θ formulas below, produces the appropriate bracketing by projecting a new word above each proclitic and relocating each proclitic's sibling to the new word constituent.

$$
\begin{aligned}
\delta_1(x) = \delta_2(x) = \theta_{(@,0)}(x) &= \\
\theta_{(@,1)}(x) = \theta_{(\omega,2)}(x) &= \circ_p(x) \\
\theta_{(\lhd_1,0,1)}(x,y) = \theta_{(\lhd_1,1,2)}(x,y) &= \circ_p(x) \wedge x = y \\
\theta_{(\lhd_0,1,0)}(x,y) &= \circ_p(x) \wedge x \lhd_1 y \\
\theta_{(\lhd_0,0,0)}(x,y) = \theta_{(\lhd_1,0,0)}(x,y) &= [etc]
\end{aligned}
$$

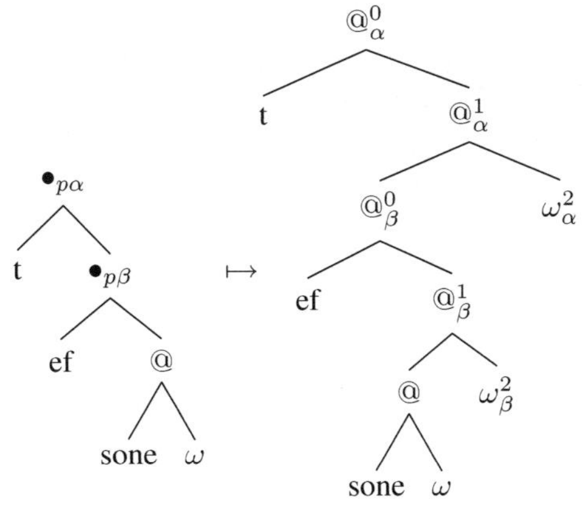

Figure 6: Local proclisis.

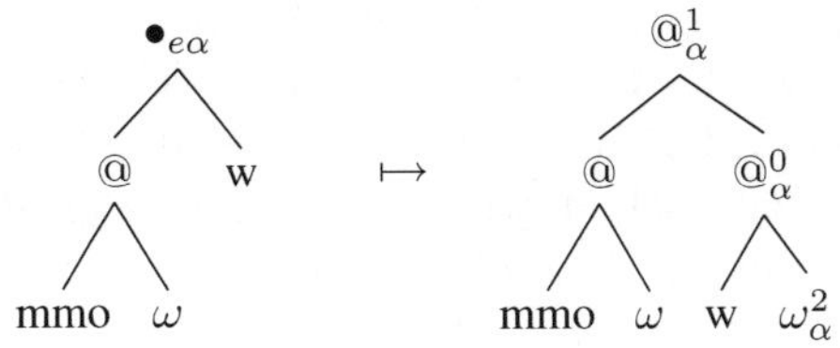

Figure 7: Local enclisis.

Figure 6 gives an example of a tree transformation effected by f_4, again with subscripts and superscripts indicating copies.

The interpretation of local enclitics proceeds similarly. A predicate $\circ_e(x)$ defines the relevant notion of locality.

$$\begin{aligned} \circ_e(x) := \bullet_e(x) \wedge \exists y(@(y) \\ \wedge x \triangleleft_0^+ y \wedge \forall z(x \triangleleft^* z \\ \wedge z \triangleleft^+ y \rightarrow \bullet_e(x))) \end{aligned}$$

The transduction $f_5 = \langle 2, \Delta, \Theta \rangle$, with Δ and Θ given by the union of the δ and θ formulas below, produces the appropriate bracketing. This transduction is more complicated than the proclitic transformation in that enclitics, right children in the source tree, must be relocated to left branches of @ nodes.

$$\begin{aligned} \delta_1(x) = \delta_2(x) = \\ \theta_{(@,0)}(x) = \theta_{(@,1)}(x) = \\ \theta_{(\omega,2)}(x) &= \circ_e(x) \\ \theta_{(\triangleleft_0,1,0)}(x,y) &= \circ_e(x) \wedge x \triangleleft_0 y \\ \theta_{(\triangleleft_1,1,0)}(x,y) &= \\ \theta_{(\triangleleft_1,0,2)}(x,y) &= \circ_e(x) \wedge x = y \\ \theta_{(\triangleleft_0,0,0)}(x,y) &= \circ_e(x) \wedge x \triangleleft_1 y \vee [etc] \\ \theta_{(\triangleleft_1,0,0)}(x,y) &= [etc] \end{aligned}$$

Figure 7 gives an example of the tree transduction specified by f_5.

3.4.2 Long-distance proclisis

Long-distance clitics, which are not locally combined with their hosts, incorporate into them in the same manner as local clitics (i.e. by transductions f_4 and f_5) but must be lowered to them to do so.

Only long-distance proclisis is relevant to the grammar fragment under consideration. A long-distance proclitic is a non-local proclitic (see Section 3.4.1 for the notion of "locality") adjacent to a word in the yield, ignoring other proclitics. Pronouns count as proclitics for this purpose, so a predicate $Pc'(x)$ including pronouns is defined. The predicate $Adj(x, y)$ expresses adjacency of x and y, and the predicate $L_p(x)$, which identifies the parents of long-distance proclitics, is defined in terms of $Adj(x, y)$.

$$\begin{aligned} Pc'(x) &:= Pc(x) \vee \mathrm{w}(x) \vee \mathrm{ef}(x) \\ Adj(x,y) &:= x \prec y \wedge \forall x'(x \prec x' \\ &\quad \wedge x' \prec y \wedge Leaf(x') \\ &\quad \rightarrow Pc'(x')) \\ L_p(x) &:= \bullet_p(x) \wedge \exists x', y(@(y) \\ &\quad \wedge x \triangleleft_0 x' \wedge Adj(x', y)) \end{aligned}$$

The parents of long-distance proclitics get attached to "goal" nodes—that is, @ nodes or other parents of long-distance proclitics—by the right child relation. The predicate $G(x)$ identifies goals, and $NG(x, y)$ identifies node x's nearest goal y.

$$\begin{aligned} G(x) &:= \bullet_p(x) \vee @(x) \\ NG(x,y) &:= x \triangleleft^+ y \wedge G(y) \wedge \forall y'(x \triangleleft^+ y' \\ &\quad \wedge G(y') \rightarrow y \prec y') \end{aligned}$$

The parent of the topmost in a path of $\bullet_p$ nodes must get attached, by whatever child relation connects that parent node to that path, to the right child of the lowest node in the path. The higher-order syntactic abbreviation $PC[i;x,y]$ specifies the relevant relation, whereby a path of $\bullet_p$ nodes begins with the ith child of x and leads to y.

$$\begin{aligned} PC[i;x,y] := &\neg \bullet_p (x) \land \neg \bullet_p (y) \\ &\land \exists x'(\bullet_p(x') \land x \lhd_i x' \\ &\land x' \lhd_1^+ y \land \forall y'(x' \lhd^* y' \\ &\land y' \lhd_1^+ y \rightarrow \bullet_p(y'))) \end{aligned}$$

The parent of a @ node targeted by a set of long-distance clitics gets attached to the highest parent of a clitic in that set. The predicate $Hi_p(x)$ identifies such highest proclitic parents. Only "maximal" @ nodes, those that are highest in the right-recursive path of @ nodes leading to an ω, are relevant; these are identified by the predicate $Max@p(x)$. The abbreviation $WC[i;x,y]$ identifies a highest $\bullet_p$ node y adjacent to a maximal @ node that is the ith child of x.

$$\begin{aligned} Hi_p(x) &:= L_p(x) \land \exists x'(x \lhd_0 x' \\ &\quad \land \forall y(y \prec x' \rightarrow \neg Pc'(y))) \\ Max@p(x) &:= @(x) \land \neg\exists y(y \lhd_1 x \land @(y)) \\ &\quad \land \exists z(x \lhd_1^+ z \land \omega(z)) \\ WC[i;x,y] &:= \exists x', y'(Max@p(x') \\ &\quad \land x \lhd_i x' \land y \lhd_0 y' \\ &\quad \land Adj(y',x') \land Hi_p(y)) \end{aligned}$$

Once these auxiliary predicates are defined, a simple MSO transduction $f_6 = \langle 0, \Delta, \Theta \rangle$ meeting the specifications given above can be defined by the union of the following formulas.

$$\begin{aligned} \theta_{\lhd_1}(x,y) = &\bullet_p (x) \land NG(x,y) \\ &\lor PC[1;x,y] \lor WC[1;x,y] \lor [etc] \\ \theta_{\lhd_0}(x,y) = &PC[0;x,y] \lor WC[0;x,y] \lor [etc] \end{aligned}$$

Figure 8 gives an example of the transduction specified by f_6. The transduction f_4 can be composed with f_6 to produce the appropriate constituency for the lowered proclitics.

3.4.3 Second-position clisis

There is little substantive difference between long-distance proclitics and 2P clitics—both arrive in their position by a "lowering" transformation that targets @ nodes. The transductions

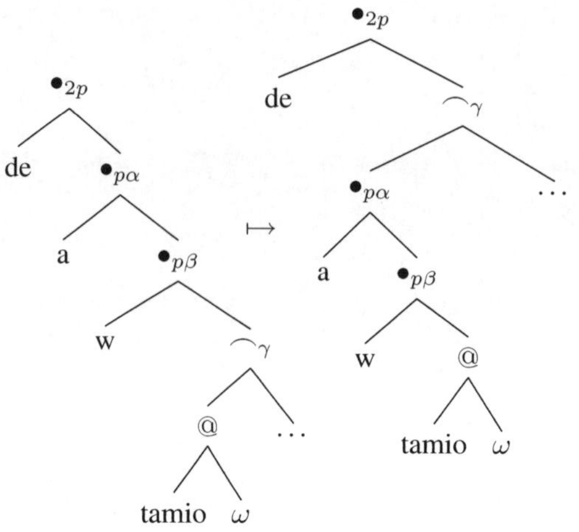

Figure 8: Long-distance proclisis, part 1: lowering.

already defined can be recycled, essentially unchanged, to derive 2P clisis.

Assume a lowering transduction f_6' identical to f_6 except operating on $\bullet_{2p}$ nodes. The resulting lowered 2P clitics, which are in a "proclitic" configuration, can then be "rotated" and relabeled as enclitics. The MSO transduction $f_7 = \langle 0, \Delta, \Theta \rangle$ given by the union of the following formulas produces this transformation.

$$\begin{aligned} \theta_{\bullet_e}(x) &= \bullet_{2p} (x) \\ \theta_{\lhd_0}(x,y) &= \neg \bullet_{2p} (x) \land x \lhd_0 y \\ &\quad \lor \bullet_{2p}(x) \land x \lhd_1 y \\ \theta_{\lhd_1}(x,y) &= \neg \bullet_{2p} (x) \land x \lhd_1 y \\ &\quad \lor \bullet_{2p}(x) \land x \lhd_0 y \end{aligned}$$

The local enclisis transduction f_5 is then applied to incorporate the 2P clitics into their hosts. An example transformation effected by the transduction $f_5 \circ f_7 \circ f_6'$ is shown in Figure 3.4.3.

3.5 Algorithmic implementation

No automaton compiler for MSO transductions exists, and the non-elementary complexity of the MSO-to-automaton translation procedure ensures that the development of a practical compiler will be a difficult undertaking. The most convenient algorithmic implementation of the above analysis is therefore an indirect one: an extensionally equivalent algorithm constructed in an expressively equivalent transduction framework.

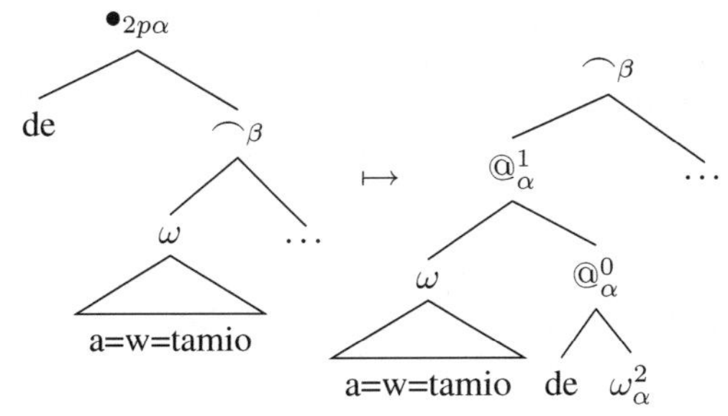

Figure 9: Second position clisis.

Second-order Abstract Categorial Grammar (Kanazawa, 2009b) is one such framework, equivalent to MSO in tree-transforming power (Kanazawa, 2009a). ACG tree transductions, which are expressed as linear λ-term homomorphisms and thus have the same complexity as linear λ-term normalization, can be implemented in Haskell in the manner of Kiselyov and Shan (2010). A function extensionally equivalent to that defined logically above can be defined in a simple ACG consisting of a composed pair of homomorphisms and implemented in Haskell in a pair of type classes.

4 Discussion and conclusion

The analysis of Sahidic Coptic 2P clitics in terms of prosodic constituency and tree transformation given above successfully accounts for the alternation shown in sentences (2) and (3). It promises to scale to a larger fragment of Coptic grammar, accommodating the addition of clitic main verbs and direct objects without further ado. The general approach also promises to extend straightforwardly to other languages with 2P clitics, such as Russian and Hittite. Since the general technique of MSO transduction underlying the analysis applies to all tree-deriving grammar formalisms, richer grammatical backbones than CFG can be deployed as necessary.

This transductive analysis is in line with a nascent convergence in perspectives on restrictive formal syntax. The mildly context-sensitive languages, polynomially parseable languages containing limited cross-serial dependencies such as those induced by 2P clitics, have received a new logical characterization in light of the past decade's surge of interest in disentangling derivations from their interpretations.[6] Mildly context-sensitive languages are the images of recognizable tree languages under monadic second-order transductions.[7] This generalizes not only string-generating formalisms like linear context-free rewriting systems (Vijay-Shanker et al., 1987; Weir, 1992) but also context-free languages of graphs (Engelfriet and Maneth, 2000) and linear λ-terms (Kanazawa, 2009a; Kanazawa, 2010).[8]

This perspective suggests a modular approach to framework revision in the face of problematic natural language phenomena. Transductive interpretations are an integral, if not universally recognized, component of restrictive grammar frameworks. Hence, to meet new descriptive challenges such as those posed by 2P clitics, it is natural to extend those frameworks' interpretive components by means of MSO rather than rebuilding them from scratch.

No software toolkit for MSO transduction comparable to the XFST toolkit for regular expressions (Beesley and Karttunen, 2003) or the MONA toolkit for MSO (Henriksen et al., 1995) presently exists, however. Nevertheless, MSO is an excellent candidate for a high-level specification language for tree transformations, promising to play the same role for tree transduction that languages such as XFST play for string transduction. MSO meanwhile serves the useful purpose of providing a denotational check on the complexity of tree transformation algorithms.

Acknowledgments

Many thanks to John Hale, Sarah Murray, Michael Weiss, and three anonymous reviewers for their valuable comments. Thanks also to Chung-chieh Shan, Chris Barker, Greg Kobele, Makoto Kanazawa, and Zoltán Varjú for their conversation and inspiration. This research was supported by the Social Sciences and Humanities Research Council.

[6] See for instance Michaelis et al. (2000), de Groote (2001), Ranta (2002), Morawietz (2003), Muskens (2003), and Pollard (2008), among many others.

[7] See Kolb et al. (2003) for an application of this perspective to the purely syntactic crossing dependencies of Dutch and Swiss German noted by a reviewer.

[8] Closely related perspectives can be found in the frameworks of second-order Abstract Categorial Grammar and Koller & Kuhlmann (2011)'s "interpreted regular tree grammar" paradigm.

References

Alexandra Y. Aikhenvald. 2003. Typological parameters for the study of clitics, with special reference to Tariana. In Robert M. W. Dixon and Alexandra Y. Aikhenvald, editors, *Word: a Cross-Linguistic Typology*, pages 42–78. Cambridge University Press, Cambridge.

Stephen R. Anderson. 2005. *Aspects of the Theory of Clitics*. Oxford University Press, Oxford.

Emmon Bach. 1987. Some generalizations of categorial grammars. In Walter J. Savitch, Emmon Bach, William Marsh, and Gila Safran-Naveh, editors, *The Formal Complexity of Natural Language*, pages 251–279. D. Reidel, Dordrecht.

Kenneth R. Beesley and Lauri Karttunen. 2003. *Finite State Morphology*. CSLI Publications, Stanford.

Roderick Bloem and Joost Engelfriet. 2000. A comparison of tree transductions defined by monadic second order logic and by attribute grammars. *Journal of Computer and System Sciences*, 6(1):1–50.

Tina Bögel, Miriam Butt, Ronald M. Kaplan, Tracy Holloway King, and John T. Maxwell. 2010. Second position and the prosody-syntax interface. In Miriam Butt and Tracy Holloway King, editors, *Proceedings of the LFG10 Conference*, pages 107–126.

Hubert Comon, Max Dauchet, Remi Gilleron, Christof Löding, Florent Jacquemard, Denis Lugiez, Sophie Tison, and Marc Tommasi. 2007. Tree automata techniques and applications. Available at: http://www.grappa.univ-lille3.fr/tata.

Bruno Courcelle and Joost Engelfriet. 2012. Graph structure and monadic second-order logic: a language theoretic approach. In press.

Bruno Courcelle. 1991. The monadic second-order logic of graphs V: on closing the gap between definability and recognizability. *Theoretical Computer Science*, 80:153–202.

Philippe de Groote. 2001. Towards abstract categorial grammars. In *Association for Computational Linguistics, 39th Annual Meeting*, pages 148–155.

Joost Engelfriet and Sebastian Maneth. 1999. Macro tree transducers, attribute grammars, and MSO definable tree translations. *Information and Computation*, 154:34–91.

Joost Engelfriet and Sebastian Maneth. 2000. Tree languages generated by context-free graph grammars. In Hartmut Ehrig, editor, *Graph Transformation*, pages 15–29, Berlin and Heidelberg. Springer Verlag.

Joost Engelfriet, Eric Lilin, and Andreas Maletti. 2009. Extended multi bottom-up tree transducers: Composition and decomposition. *Acta Informatica*, 46:561–590.

Zoltán Fülöp, Armin Kühnemann, and Heiko Vogler. 2004. A bottom-up characterization of deterministic top-down tree transducers with regular look-ahead. *Information Processing Letters*, 91:57–67.

Aaron Halpern. 1995. *On the Placement and Morphology of Clitics*. CSLI Publications, Stanford.

Jesper G. Henriksen, Jakob Jensen, Michael Jørgensen, Nils Klarlund, Robert Paige, Theis Rauhe, and Anders Sandholm. 1995. MONA: Monadic second-order logic in practice. *Lecture Notes in Computer Science*, 1019:89–110.

Sharon Inkelas and Draga Zec. 1990. Prosodically constrained syntax. In Sharon Inkelas and Draga Zec, editors, *The phonology–syntax connection*, pages 365–378. University of Chicago Press, Chicago.

Makoto Kanazawa. 2009a. A lambda calculus characterization of MSO definable tree transductions. Talk given at the 10th Asian Logic Conference.

Makoto Kanazawa. 2009b. Second-order abstract categorial grammars. Manuscript.

Makoto Kanazawa. 2010. Second-order abstract categorial grammars as hyperedge replacement grammars. *Journal of Language, Logic, and Information*, 19(2):137–161.

Oleg Kiselyov and Chung-chieh Shan. 2010. Lambda: the ultimate syntax-semantics interface. NASSLLI 2010 course notes.

Hans-Peter Kolb, Jens Michaelis, Uwe Mönnich, and Frank Morawietz. 2003. An operational and denotational approach to non-context-freeness. *Theoretical Computer Science*, 293:261–289.

Alexander Koller and Marco Kuhlmann. 2011. A generalized view on parsing and translation. In *Proceedings of the 12th International Conference on Parsing Technologies*, pages 2–11.

Andreas Maletti. 2011. Tree transformations and dependencies. *Lecture Notes in Computer Science*, 6878:1–20.

Jens Michaelis, Uwe Mönnich, and Frank Morawietz. 2000. Derivational minimalism in two regular and logical steps. In *Proceedings of TAG+ 5*.

Frank Morawietz. 2003. *Two-Step Approaches to Natural Language Formalisms*. Mouton de Gruyter, Berlin and New York.

Reinhard Muskens. 2003. Language, lambdas, and logic. In Richard T. Oehrle and Geert-Jan Kruijff, editors, *Resource sensitivity in binding and anaphora*, pages 23–54. Kluwer, Dordrecht.

Marina Nespor and Irene Vogel. 1986. *Prosodic Phonology*. Foris, Dordrecht.

Tito Orlandi. 2004. Towards a computational grammar of Sahidic Coptic. In Jacques van der Vliet and Mat Immerzeel, editors, *Coptic studies on the threshold of a new millennium*, pages 125–130, Leuven. Peeters.

Carl Pollard. 2008. An introduction to convergent grammar. Manuscript.

Aarne Ranta. 2002. Grammatical Framework. *Journal of Functional Programming*, 14:145–189.

Chris Reintges. 2004. *Coptic Egyptian (Sahidic Dialect)*. Rüdiger Köppe Verlag, Köln.

Elisabeth Selkirk. 1986. On derived domains in sentence phonology. *Phonology Yearbook*, 3:371–405.

K. Vijay-Shanker, David J. Weir, and Aravind K. Joshi. 1987. Characterizing structural descriptions produced by various grammatical formalisms. In *Proceedings of the 25th annual meeting on Association for Computational Linguistics*.

Jacob Wackernagel. 1892. Über ein Gesetz der indogermanischen Wortstellung. *Indogermanische Forschungen*, 1:333–436.

David J. Weir. 1992. Linear context-free rewriting systems and deterministic tree-walking transducers. In *Proceedings of the 30th annual meeting on Association for Computational Linguistics*.

Draga Zec. 2005. Prosodic differences among function words. *Phonology*, 22:77–112.

Arnold M. Zwicky. 1977. On clitics. Manuscript.

Author Index

Association for Computational Linguistics
209 N. Eighth Street
Stroudsburg, Pennsylvania 18360

CURRAN ASSOCIATES INC
proceedings.com